creating the *happiest* of HOLIDAYS
BOOK 2

LEISURE ARTS, INC.
Little Rock, Arkansas

EDITORIAL STAFF

Editor-in-Chief: **Susan White Sullivan**
Designer Relations Director: **Debra Nettles**
Craft Publications Director: **Cheryl Johnson**
Art Publications Director: **Rhonda Shelby**
Special Projects Director: **Susan Frantz Wiles**
Senior Prepress Director: **Mark Hawkins**
Technical Editor: **Mary Sullivan Hutcheson**
Contributing Editors: **Laura Siar Bertram, Linda Daley,
Sarah J. Green, Lois J. Long, and Jane Kenner Prather**
Contributing Test Kitchen Assistant: **Rose Glass Klein**
Editorial Writer: **Susan McManus Johnson**
Designers: **Kim Hamblin, Anne Pulliam Stocks,
Lori Wenger, and Becky Werle**
Art Category Manager: **Lora Puls**
Lead Graphic Artist: **Amy Temple**
Graphic Artist: **Jacob Casleton**
Production Artist: **Janie Wright**
Imaging Technicians: **Brian Hall,
Stephanie Johnson, and Mark R. Potter**
Photography Manager: **Katherine Laughlin**
Lead Contributing Photo Stylist: **Christy Myers**
Contributing Photo Stylist: **Sondra Daniel**
Publishing Systems Administrator: **Becky Riddle**
Publishing Systems Assistants: **Clint Hanson and Robert Young**

BUSINESS STAFF

Vice President and Chief Operations Officer:
Tom Siebenmorgen
Director of Finance and Administration: **Laticia Mull Dittrich**
Vice President, Sales and Marketing: **Pam Stebbins**
National Accounts Director: **Martha Adams**
Sales and Services Director: **Margaret Reinold**
Information Technology Director: **Hermine Linz**
Controller: **Francis Caple**
Vice President, Operations: **Jim Dittrich**
Comptroller, Operations: **Rob Thieme**
Retail Customer Service Manager: **Stan Raynor**
Print Production Manager: **Fred F. Pruss**

CREDITS

We want to especially thank Mark Mathews of
Mark Mathews Photography and Ken West of
Ken West Photography for their excellent work.

We would like to recognize Lion Brand® Yarn and Red Heart®
Yarn for providing yarn and thread.

Special thanks go to Marianna Crowder
for crocheting the snowflake models.

Library of Congress Control Number: 2010923986
ISBN-13: 978-1-60900-012-7
1 0 9 8 7 6 5 4 3

creating the *happiest* of HOLIDAYS

No matter how busy you are, the biggest *celebration* of the year can also be your most enjoyable. To help you create *beautiful* memories of *Christmas*, we've gathered dozens of *delicious* recipes, ideas for wondrous *gifts* and *wrappings*, and plenty of ways to make your home *sparkle* with all the *happiness* of the season!

Contents

creative *gift giving* for the HOLIDAYS

Make their Christmas very merry with *keepsakes and accessories* you create. Quick and easy or truly artistic, there are ideas here for everyone on your list. No time to make the simplest gift? Purchased items become special when presented in *one-of-a-kind wrappings!*

They say that Christmas is for kids, so why not let the youngsters in your house dive into the merriment of making really cool gifts and decorations? Clear off a table and set up the supplies to assemble such thoughtful things as a Snowman Bell Ornament or Tea Towel Apron!

Snowman Bell Ornament

• 35 mm jingle bell • white acrylic paint and paintbrush • $1/8$" dia. circle punch • orange and black craft foam • craft glue • white cloth-wrapped floral wire • wire cutters • hot glue gun • two $1/4$" dia. green pom-poms • red yarn

1. Paint the bell white. For the eyes and mouth, punch 7 black foam circles. For the nose, cut a $3/8$" long orange foam carrot shape. Holding the bell upside down, glue the foam pieces to the bell.

2. For the ear muffs, hot glue a $2^{1}/_{2}$" wire length to the bell sides. Glue a pom-pom over each end of the wire. Loop a yarn length through the ear muffs for a hanger. ❀

Tea Towel Apron

• water-soluble fabric marker • tea towel (ours is $18^{1}/_{4}$" x $26^{1}/_{4}$") • $2^{1}/_{2}$ yds of $5/8$"w twill tape • safety pin • liquid fray preventative

1. Referring to **Fig. 1**, mark the apron top and side edges on the towel. Connect the marks and trim along the drawn lines.
2. For the casings, press $1/2$", then 1" to the wrong side along the cut edges. Topstitch in place.
3. Beginning at the top, use the safety pin to thread a twill tape end through each casing. Trim the ends and apply liquid fray preventative. ❀

Fig. 1

Chenille Stem Friends

Santa

- cardstock • 2¹/₂" dia. circle punch • pinking shears • 2 black 11 mm wood beads • craft glue • 6 mm white and nylon glitter red chenille stems • white bump chenille stem • 6 mm twisted chenille stem for candy cane • utility scissors • ³/₄" dia. wood bead for Santa's head • ¹/₂" white pom-pom • 3 mm red pom-pom • 4 mm wiggle eyes

1. For the base, punch a circle from cardstock; pink the edges. Glue the black beads about 1" apart on the circle; let this dry while you make Santa.
2. Trim 2 red stems to 8". Place the stems next to each other. Starting 2" from the top, twist the stems together for 1¹/₂", forming the body; pull the stems slightly apart at both the top and the bottom.
3. To form the legs, fold each bottom stem in half and twist back up toward the body (*Fig. 1*).
4. Thread the ³/₄" dia. head bead onto another red stem for about 1". Loosely wrap the longer stem end around the body to form Santa's coat (*Fig. 2*); trim any excess.
5. For the hat, wrap a 4" red stem length around the head and 1" stem end, tapering into a cone shape as it reaches the top; trim any excess.
6. For the arms, bend the top stems into place. Wrap white stem lengths around the "sleeves" and around the hat lower edge. Glue pieces as necessary. Glue the white pom-pom to the hat.
7. To form the beard, cut a bump stem length that has 2 bumps, one at each end. Wrap the stem around the head and twist the bumps together. Glue the eyes and pom-pom nose to the head.
8. Shape a 3" twisted stem length into a candy cane and glue to Santa's hand.
9. Glue the legs into the beads on the cardstock base. ❄

Reindeer

- cardstock • 2¹/₂" dia. circle punch • pinking shears • 4 black 11 mm wood beads • craft glue • 15 mm brown chenille stems • utility scissors • 6 mm tan chenille stems • 5 mm wiggle eyes • 5 mm red pom-pom

1. For the base, punch a circle from cardstock; pink the edges. Glue the black beads on the circle, spacing them for the reindeer's legs; let this dry while you make the reindeer.
2. Cut three 5" brown stem lengths. Shape one into the head, neck, and body; bend the other 2 in half and twist around the body for the legs (*Fig. 3*). Loosely wrap a 7" brown stem length around the body.
3. To form the antlers, twist a 2" tan stem length around each end of a 5" tan stem length. Twist the antlers around the top of the head.
4. Glue the eyes and pom-pom nose to the head. Glue the legs into the beads on the cardstock base. ❄

Fig. 1

Fig. 2

Fig. 3

What fun the kids will have as they twist Chenille Stem Friends into shape!
Beads, pom-poms, and moving eyes make these cute little figures come to life.

With a little help from an adult, children can easily make colorful Bird Feeders. And it may be a good idea to have one or two extra candy bars on hand for young crafters who make colorful Candy Bar Wraps!

Bird Feeders
• lard • chunky peanut butter
• birdseed • large rounded fruit (oranges, limes, pomegranates, lemons) • cranberries • large-eye long needle • twine

1. To make the birdseed ball treats, measure out 2 parts lard, 1 part peanut butter, and 1 part birdseed. Microwave the lard and peanut butter on HIGH in 1 minute increments until it's soft enough to mix together completely. Stir in the birdseed and refrigerate until firm. Once the mixture is firm, form balls somewhat smaller than the large fruit. Refrigerate until ready to assemble.

2. To assemble the feeders, cut the large fruit in half. Thread the needle with a long length of twine. Referring to **Fig. 1** and leaving a hanging loop at the top, thread the twine through the fruit, a birdseed ball, a berry, and then back through all; securely knot the ends at the bottom.

3. Hang outside immediately or refrigerate until ready to place outdoors. ❀

Fig. 1

Candy Bar Wrap

• candy bar (ours are 2¼" x 5½" each) • scrapbook paper • double-sided tape • cardstock • circle punches (ours measure 2" and 2½" dia.) • rub-on letters

Cut scrapbook paper to fit around the candy bar (we cut a 5½" x 6¼" piece). Wrap the paper around the bar and tape in place. Layer scrapbook paper and cardstock circles; personalize with the rub-on letters. Tape the tag to the wrapped candy bar. ❊

Easy-sew gifts like a Place Mat Apron and Fleece Stockings are as delightful to make as they are to share. Kids can also help trim the tree with clever Craft-Spoon Poinsettias.

Place Mat Apron

- place mat • 2$\frac{1}{2}$ yds ribbon for ties • clear nylon thread • twill tape, rickrack, and ball fringe trims
- 12" x 6$\frac{1}{2}$" fabric piece for pocket
- liquid fray preventative

Use clear nylon thread for all sewing.

1. Center and stitch the tie ribbon about 1" from one long place mat edge.
2. Wrapping the ends to the back, straight stitch or zigzag stitch the twill tape and rickrack trims to the apron.
3. Press all edges of the pocket fabric $\frac{1}{4}$" to the wrong side twice. Wrapping the ends to the back, layer and zigzag stitch the twill tape and ball fringe on the pocket top edge.
4. Pin the pocket on the apron and topstitch in place along the side and bottom edges. Topstitch the pocket down the center to create 2 pockets. Apply liquid fray preventative to the tie ends. ❈

Fleece Stockings

• 1/2 yd fleece for each stocking • fleece scraps for appliqués • embroidery floss • fabric glue • ball fringe

Read Embroidery Stitches, page 149, before beginning your stocking. Use 3 strands of floss for all embroidery stitches.

1. Enlarge the patterns, page 156, to 151%. Using the patterns, cut 2 stockings (1 in reverse) and the desired appliqués from fleece.
2. Work *Blanket Stitches* to attach the appliqués to a stocking piece. For the snowman, add *French Knot* buttons and facial features; glue on the nose. For the scarf, knot a 1/2" x 9" fleece strip in the center and cut fringe at the ends. Tack to the snowman.
3. Matching the wrong sides and leaving the top edge open, work *Blanket Stitches* to join the stocking pieces. Glue the ball fringe along the stocking top. For the hanger, cut a 3/4" x 6" fleece strip. Fold the strip in half and glue or sew into the stocking top corner. ❄

Craft-Spoon Poinsettia

• utility scissors • 8 red and 3 green craft spoons • low-temp glue gun • assorted white and yellow beads • clear nylon thread

1. Cut the handles from 4 red spoons and 3 green spoons; discard the handles. Glue each red spoon half to the handle of a whole red spoon (*Fig. 1*).
2. Glue a pair of red spoons together to form a cross; repeat with the remaining pair. Layer and glue the red spoon crosses and green spoon halves to form a poinsettia.
3. Glue beads to the poinsettia center. Glue a nylon thread hanger to the poinsettia back. ❄

Fig. 1

The fun of making presents is applying a bit of unique flair to each one. For instance, the six Sparkling Snowflakes on this wreath are all made from the same simple pattern, but were finished to look entirely different! Let all the gift ideas on these pages inspire your creativity.

Sparkling Snowflakes
approx finished size:
5" (12.5 cm) dia. each

• bedspread weight
cotton thread (size 5),
approximately 10 yards
(9 meters) for each snowflake
• steel crochet hook, size 2
(2.25 mm) or size needed for
gauge • terry towel • fabric
stiffener • resealable plastic
bag • blocking board or ironing
board • plastic wrap • paper
towels • rust-proof pins
• toothbrush • spray adhesive
• iridescent fine crystal glitter
• clear nylon thread

GAUGE: 38 chs = 5" (12.75 cm)

SNOWFLAKE
Ch 6; join with slip st to form a ring.
Rnd 1 (Right side): ★ Ch 20, slip st in ring, ch 26, slip st in 20th ch from hook, (ch 20, slip st in same ch) twice, ch 6, slip st in ring; repeat from ★ 5 times **more**; finish off.

FINISHING
Follow all steps for each snowflake.
1. Use a mild detergent and warm water to wash the snowflake; rinse thoroughly. Roll in a terry towel, gently pressing out the excess moisture. For best stiffening results, allow the snowflake to dry completely.
2. Pour fabric stiffener into the plastic bag; place the snowflake in the stiffener. Press out the air and seal the bag. Work the stiffener into the snowflake; allow the snowflake to soak for several hours.
3. Enlarge the desired snowflake pattern, page 155, to 200%. Place the pattern on the blocking board and cover with plastic wrap.
4. Remove the snowflake from the stiffener; squeeze the snowflake gently and blot with paper towels to remove the excess stiffener.
5. Place the snowflake right side up on the pattern. Shape the snowflake over the pattern, pinning in place. Allow to dry. Use the toothbrush to remove excess dried stiffener from the open areas of the snowflake.
6. Working in a well-ventilated area, spray the snowflake with adhesive and sprinkle glitter over the snowflake. Shake off the excess glitter and add a nylon thread hanger. ❄

gifts for everyone * 15

V-Stitch Ripple Crochet Afghan

finished size: 45¹/₂" x 60" (115.5 cm x 152.5 cm) ◖◼◻◻ **EASY**

- Super Bulky Weight Yarn **6** (SUPER BULKY)
  [6 ounces, 106 yards (170 grams, 97 meters) per ball]

black – 6 balls	scrap yarn – 7 balls total (we
green – 3 balls	used lt orange, orange, lt green, and red)

- Crochet hook, size N (9 mm) **or** size needed for gauge

GAUGE: From point to point = 6¹/₂" (16.5 cm)
Gauge swatch: 13"w x 4"h (33 cm x 10 cm)
Ch 48.
Work same as Afghan for 3 rows.

STITCH GUIDE

V-Stitch (abbreviated V-St)
(Dc, ch 1, dc) in st or sp indicated.

Beginning Decrease
Make a slip knot on hook, YO, holding YO with index finger, insert hook in first dc, YO and pull up a loop (3 loops on hook), YO and draw through 2 loops on hook, YO, insert hook in next ch-1 sp, YO and pull up a loop, YO and draw through 2 loops on hook, YO and draw through all 3 loops on hook (**counts as one dc**).

Decrease
† YO, insert hook in next ch-1 sp, YO and pull up loop, YO and draw through 2 loops on hook †, skip next 3 dc, repeat from † to † once, YO and draw through all 3 loops on hook (**counts as one dc**).

Ending Decrease
YO, insert hook in next ch-1 sp, YO and pull up a loop, YO and draw through 2 loops on hook, skip next dc, YO, insert hook in last dc, YO and pull up a loop, YO and draw through 2 loops on hook, YO and draw through all 3 loops on hook (**counts as one dc**).

Picot

Ch 2, hdc in second ch from hook.

Sc Decrease

Pull up a loop in next 2 chs, YO and draw through all 3 loops on hook.

AFGHAN

With black, ch 158.

Row 1 (Wrong side): Dc in fifth ch from hook (**4 skipped chs count as first dc plus one skipped ch**), (skip next 2 chs, work V-st in next ch) 3 times, ch 3, work V-St in next ch, (skip next 2 chs, work V-St in next ch) twice, ★ (skip next 2 chs, YO, insert hook in next ch, YO and pull up a loop, YO and draw through 2 loops on hook) twice, YO and draw through all 3 loops on hook (**counts as one dc**), (skip next 2 chs, work V-St in next ch) 3 times, ch 3, work V-St in next ch, (skip next 2 chs, work V-St in next ch) twice; repeat from ★ across to last 5 chs, skip next 2 chs, † YO, insert hook in next ch, YO and pull up a loop, YO and draw through 2 loops on hook †, skip next ch, repeat from † to † once, YO and draw through all 3 loops on hook (**counts as one dc**); finish off.

*Note: Loop a short piece of yarn around **back** of any stitch on Row 1 to mark **right** side.*

Row 2: With **right** side facing, join green with beginning decrease, work V-St in next 2 V-Sts (ch-1 sp), work (V-St, ch 3, V-St) in next ch-3 sp, work V-St in next 2 V-Sts, ★ decrease, work V-St in next 2 V-Sts, work (V-St, ch 3, V-St) in next ch-3 sp, work V-St in next 2 V-Sts; repeat from ★ across to last V-St, work ending decrease; finish off.

Row 3: With **wrong** side facing, join black with beginning decrease, work V-St in next 2 V-Sts, work (V-St, ch 3, V-St) in next ch-3 sp, work V-St in next 2 V-Sts, ★ decrease, work V-St in next 2 V-Sts, work (V-St, ch 3, V-St) in next ch-3 sp, work V-St in next 2 V-Sts; repeat from ★ across to last V-St, work ending decrease; finish off.

Row 4: With scrap color, repeat Row 2.

Row 5: With scrap color, repeat Row 3.

Row 6: With scrap color, repeat Row 2.

Row 7: Repeat Row 3.

Rows 8-44: Repeat Rows 2-7, 6 times; then repeat Row 2 once **more**.

Last Row: Repeat Row 3; do **not** finish off.

Edging: Ch 1, turn; sc in first dc, work Picot, (sc in next V-St, work Picot) 3 times, (sc, work Picot, sc) in next ch-3 sp, (work Picot, sc in next V-St) 3 times, † skip next dc, sc in next dc, (sc in next V-St, work Picot) 3 times, (sc, work Picot, sc) in next ch-3 sp, (work Picot, sc in next V-St) 3 times †; repeat from † to † across to last 2 dc, work Picot, skip next dc, (slip st, ch 2, dc) in last dc; working in end of rows, skip first row, (slip st, ch 2, dc) in top of dc on next row and each row across; working in free loops of beginning ch, sc in base of first dc, work Picot, sc in next sp, (work Picot, sc in next sp) 3 times, work sc decrease, (sc in next sp, work Picot) 3 times, ★ (sc, work Picot, sc) in next sp, (work Picot, sc in next sp) 3 times, work sc decrease, (sc in next sp, work Picot) 3 times; repeat from ★ across to last sp, sc in last sp, work Picot, (slip st, ch 2, dc) in base of last dc; working in end of rows, (slip st, ch 2, dc) in top of dc on same row and each row across to last row, skip last row; join with slip st to first sc, finish off.

Design by Anne Halliday. ❊

Super bulky yarn and a large crochet hook will have your fingers flying through the creation of this colorful V-Stitch afghan.

Apron

- several coordinating fabrics (we used 5 fabrics) • 1^1/$_2$ yds fabric for lining • rickrack and ribbons for trims, plus 4 yds of 1^1/$_2$"w ribbon for ties • clear nylon thread • extra-wide double-fold bias tape

For all sewing, match the right sides and raw edges and use a ^{1}/$_2$" seam allowance, unless otherwise stated.

1. For the bib front, cut a 13" x 13" fabric piece. Mark a point 1" in from each top corner. Draw a line connecting the dots to the lower corners *(Fig. 1)*. Cut along the drawn lines. Repeat with the lining fabric.

2. Use nylon thread to zigzag stitch ribbon and rickrack to the bib front. Sew the bib front and lining pieces together along the bottom edge only. Turn the bib right side out and press. Baste along the side and top edges.

3. For the neck ties, baste a 27" ribbon length to each corner on the lining side of the bib top, about ^{3}/$_4$" in from the edges. Insert the bib raw edges into the folds of the bias tape; topstitch in place, mitering at the corners and catching the neck ties in the stitching.

4. For the skirt front, sew 35" long fabric strips together (of varying widths). We used 7 fabric strips for our 22" skirt. Zigzag stitch ribbons and rickrack to the skirt. Cut a lining fabric piece the same size as the skirt. Leaving an opening for turning, sew the skirt lining to the skirt. Clip the corners, turn right side out, press, and sew the opening closed. Refer to **Fig. 2** to pleat the top of the skirt.

5. Overlapping about ^{1}/$_2$", center and sew the bib on the skirt. Center and topstitch the remaining ribbon tie on the apron. ❊

Fig. 1

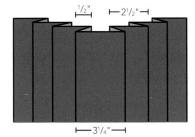

Fig. 2

For all the cooks you know, make Aprons in their favorite colors.

Mattress-Style Floor Pillow

• 1¹⁄₈ yards of 54"w heavyweight fabric • two 10" grosgrain ribbon lengths • 24" square pillow form • quilt batting • embroidery floss

For all sewing, match the right sides and raw edges and use a ¹⁄₂" seam allowance, unless otherwise stated.

1. Cut two 26" squares and four 6" x 26" fabric strips.
2. For each handle, center and securely sew the ends of one ribbon length on the right side of one 6" fabric strip, folding the cut ends of the ribbon to the wrong side (see photo, right).
3. Sew the 6" strips together along the short ends, creating the box sides of the pillow. Sew the box sides to the pillow top and bottom, leaving an opening for turning and stuffing; turn right side out.
4. Wrap the pillow form in batting; loosely tack the batting together. Insert the pillow form into the pillow and sew the opening closed.
5. To create the pillow edging, use 6 strands of floss to work *Running Stitches*, page 149, ³⁄₄" inside the edges of the pillow. To tuft the pillow, run floss lengths through the pillow twice and knot at the top. ✳

Pajama Pants

• pajama pants to use as a pattern • large piece of paper for pattern • three coordinating fabrics for pants and cuffs (we used a diagonal plaid for pants, a light-colored stripe for cuff facing, and a solid for cuff trim) • lightweight fusible interfacing • ¹⁄₂"w twill tape for drawstring • large safety pin

For all sewing, match the right sides and raw edges and use a ¹⁄₂" seam allowance.

1. Match the outside leg edges and fold the pajama pants in half. For a pattern, stretch the waistband of the pants (if necessary) and draw around the pants on the paper. Add 1¹⁄₂" at the top, ³⁄₄" on each side, and 4¹⁄₂" at the hem for your cutting lines (*Fig. 1*).
2. Using the pattern, cut 4 fabric pieces (2 in reverse).

Fig. 1

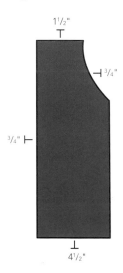

3. Sew the pieces together in pairs along the outer side edges. Sew each inseam.

4. Turn one leg right side out and slip it inside the other, aligning the seams *(Fig. 2)*. Sew the crotch seam and pull the inside leg out.

5. For the waistline casing, press the top edge of the pants ¹/₂", then 1" to the wrong side; unfold. Make 2 buttonholes on the front of the pants just below the bottom fold line, stitching through one layer of fabric (for added stability, fuse a bit of interfacing to that area of the casing before working the buttonholes). Refold the casing and sew along the bottom folded edge. Cut the twill tape 20" longer than the boy's waist measurement. Use the safety pin to thread the twill tape through the casing. Knot the ends. Turn the pants right side out.

6. Measure around the bottom edge of one pant leg; add 1". For the solid cuff trim, cut a 1³/₄" wide strip the determined measurement. For the striped cuff facing, cut a 5" wide piece the determined measurement.

7. Matching the short ends, sew the cuff facing and the cuff trim pieces into rings. Matching the wrong sides and long edges, press the cuff trim piece in half. Referring to **Fig. 3** and sandwiching the cuff trim between the pant leg and the cuff facing, sew the cuff pieces to the pant leg. Press the cuff facing raw edge ¹/₂" to the wrong side. Turn the pants wrong side out.

8. Fold the facing right side out and topstitch the pressed edge in place on the inside of the pant leg. Turn the pants right side out. Fold the cuff up and tack at the sides.

9. Repeat Steps 6-8 for the remaining cuff. ❄

Fig. 2

Fig. 3

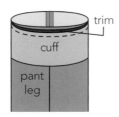

trim

cuff

pant leg

Mattress-Style Floor Pillows are surprisingly simple to sew and a fun way to add casual seating for the holidays. A child who rises early on Christmas Day will need a warm pair of Pajama Pants. They're easy to make by using an existing pair of pajama pants for a pattern. The turned-up cuff can be let down as the youngster grows.

Place Mat

finished size: 11 1/2" x 16"
• 12" x 24" fabric piece for place mat • 2 1/2" x 24" fabric strip for narrow trim • 4 1/2" x 24" fabric strip for wide trim • paper-backed fusible web • fabric scraps for holly leaves • clear nylon thread • three 1/2" dia. buttons for berries

For all sewing, match the right sides and raw edges and use a 1/2" seam allowance.

1. Matching the long edges, sew the narrow trim to the place mat fabric piece. Sew the wide trim to the narrow trim.
2. Matching the short ends, sew the place mat together, forming a tube. Press the seam allowances open. Placing the seam at the center back and leaving an opening for turning, sew the side seams (*Fig. 1*).
3. Clip the corners, turn the place mat right side out, and fold the raw edges to the inside; topstitch all the edges.
4. Enlarge the pattern, page 154, to 142%. Trace the enlarged pattern on the paper side of the fusible web 4 times; fuse to fabric scraps and cut out. Fuse, then use nylon thread to zigzag stitch the leaves to the place mat. Sew on the berry buttons. ✳

Fig. 1

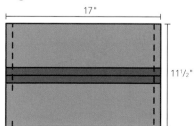

Help someone set a pretty table with an appliquéd Place Mat. For the sewing enthusiast, a merry little Snowman Pincushion is a quick gift.

Snowman Pincushion

- white, orange, red, and yellow felt • polyester fiberfill
- small buttons for eyes
- small snaps for buttons
- embroidery floss • small bag of aquarium gravel or sand • ribbon • flower and 1/4" dia. circle punch • pin

For all sewing, match raw edges and use a 1/4" seam allowance, unless otherwise stated.

1. Enlarge the patterns, page 153, to 158%. Using the patterns, cut a nose from orange felt and 2 bodies, 4 arms, and a base from white felt.
2. For each arm, sew 2 arm pieces together, leaving the straight edge open. Trim the seam allowances to 1/8". Lightly stuff with fiberfill. Baste the arms to a body piece (**Fig. 1**).

Fig. 1

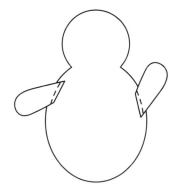

3. Leaving the bottom open, sew the body pieces together with the arms between the 2 bodies. Trim the seam allowances to 1/8".
4. Sew the nose, button eyes, and snap "buttons" on the snowman. Use 1 strand of floss to work Running Stitches, page 149, for the mouth.
5. Stuff the body with fiberfill, adding the small bag of gravel at the bottom. Whipstitch the base to the snowman bottom.
6. Tie a ribbon scarf around his neck. Layer a punched red felt flower with a punched yellow felt circle and attach to the snowman with the pin. ❄

This clever Christmas Card Tote makes it a breeze to write a few greetings whenever time allows. It keeps pens, cards, envelopes, and postage stamps all in one take-along bag.

Christmas Card Tote

• ³/₄ yd each of tote fabric, lining fabric, and heavyweight interfacing • 2⁵/₈ yds of ³/₈"w velvet ribbon • fabric glue • spray adhesive • 6¹/₂" x 10³/₄" piece of ¹/₄" thick foam core board

For all sewing, match the right sides and raw edges and use a ¹/₂" seam allowance, unless otherwise stated.

1. Cut one 12" x 23" front/back piece and two 7¹/₂" x 8¹/₄" end pieces each from tote fabric, lining, and interfacing.
2. For stability, baste the interfacing to the wrong side of each tote piece, using a ³/₈" seam allowance.
3. Mark a dot ¹/₂" in from each bottom corner of the end pieces *(Fig. 1)*. Pin one long edge of the front/back piece to one end piece *(Fig. 2)*. Sew the pieces together, stopping at the dot *(Fig. 3)*. With the needle in the fabric, pivot, then sew across the bottom to the remaining dot. Pivot and sew the remaining edge. Repeat to sew the opposite end to the front/back. Turn the tote right side out.
4. Cut two 3" x 12" handles from tote fabric. For each handle, sew the long edges together. Turn right side out and press. Center and pin the handles on the tote front and back, leaving 3" between the handle ends.
5. For the pocket, cut a 5³/₄" x 6" piece from the tote fabric. Press the top long edge of the pocket piece ¹/₄" to the wrong side twice; topstitch. Sew ribbon on the front of the pocket.
6. Press the raw edges of the pocket ¹/₄" to the wrong side. Center and pin the pocket on the lining front/back, with the top of the pocket 2¹/₂" from short edge of the lining. To add penholder loops, fold four 3" ribbon lengths in half and pin the ends under the pocket sides near the top and bottom; topstitch the pocket in place.
7. Leaving an opening at the bottom of one end for turning, sew the lining front/back to the ends; do not turn right side out. Matching the right sides, insert the tote in the lining. Sew the tote and lining together along the top edge. Turn right side out and sew the opening closed. Tuck the lining in the tote. Topstitch ¹/₂" from the top edge. Glue ribbon over the stitching on the tote and lining.
8. Working in a well-ventilated area, spray the back of a 10¹/₂" x 14³/₄" lining piece with adhesive. Center the foam core on the fabric and wrap the excess to the back. Place the covered piece in the bottom of the tote. ❋

Fig. 1

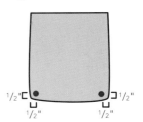

¹/₂"   ¹/₂"
¹/₂"   ¹/₂"

Fig. 2

Fig. 3

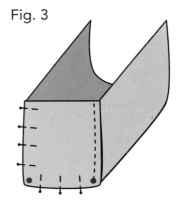

Shimmering Bracelet

- nylon-coated beading wire
- wire cutters • 2 three-strand spacer bars • crimp beads
- crimping jewelry pliers • 6 mm faceted aurora borealis beads
- 4 mm and 6 mm pearlized beads • jump rings • toggle clasp • needle-nose jewelry pliers • head pin • eye pin

finished size: approx. 6" long (adjust wire lengths in Step 1 for other sizes)

1. Cut three 16" lengths of wire.
2. Fold a wire length in half and thread it through one spacer bar loop. Slide a crimp bead onto both wires and crimp the bead (page 150). Separate the wires. For each wire, attach a crimp bead where desired; then, add a few beads and attach another crimp bead. Repeat this sequence until you only have about 2" of each wire left. Thread both ends through a crimp bead and a loop on the remaining spacer bar; then, run the wires back through the crimp bead. Crimp and trim the excess wire.
3. Repeat Step 2 with the remaining wire lengths.
4. Use jump rings (page 150) to attach the spacer bars to the clasp.
5. For the bead dangle, thread 1 bead each on the head pin and eye pin. Shape eye loops, page 150, to add the head pin to the eye pin and then to add the eye pin to one of the jump rings. ❈

The fun of receiving a Shimmering Bracelet lasts all year! Christmas décor with a bit of whimsy—the Bright Beaded Tree is truly simple to shape with an assortment of wires.

Bright Beaded Tree

- 2" square wooden block • drill and ³/₈" bit • acrylic paint and paintbrushes
- 11½" length of ³/₈" dia. dowel
- sandpaper • wood glue • cardboard
- 8-ft. length of ¹/₁₆" dia. armature wire
- wire cutters • assorted colors and diameters of wire and beaded trim (we used 20-gauge gold wire, green coated wire, purple and gold seed bead wires, and green beaded trim)
- 22-gauge rust wire • assorted beads
- needle-nose pliers • 2" rusty tin star

1. Drill a hole through the center of the block. Paint the block and dowel; then, sand the block edges. Dab glue on one end of the dowel and insert it in the block.
2. Cut an 8"-tall simple triangular tree shape from cardboard. Leaving a 3" wire tail at the bottom of the tree, wrap the armature wire randomly around the tree, wrapping loosely to allow the wire tree to be rounded. Cut away the cardboard. Center the wire tree on the dowel and wrap the wire tail tightly around the dowel.
3. Wrap the tree with the gold, green, and seed bead wires, and beaded trim. Cut a 20" length of rust wire and curl one end. Thread beads on the wire, using the pliers to coil the wire every so often. Curl the other end and wrap the strand around the tree. Repeat to add several beaded rust wire strands to the tree, using different bead combinations.
4. Wrap the star with gold wire and wire it to the tree.
5. For ornament hangers, cut several 3" gold wire lengths. Curl one end of each, add a large bead, and hook the other end to the tree. ❄

Signature Table Runner

Give a family heirloom that can be passed on for generations. Prior to Christmas, collect family members' signatures. Refer to Sizing Patterns, page 148, and enlarge the signatures to fit a table runner. Transfer the signatures to the runner with a water-soluble fabric marking pen. With 3 strands of embroidery floss, stitch each name using Stem Stitches, page 149. Each year bring out the table runner and add signatures. ✽

Modern Tree

fits an 8" x 10" frame
- background fabric • water-soluble fabric marking pen
- embroidery floss • fabric scraps • embroidery needle
- assorted coins • buttons
- cotton swab • 8" x 10" frame

Refer to Embroidery Stitches, page 149, and use 3 strands of floss for all embroidery.

1. Enlarge the pattern, page 154, to 160%. Tape the pattern, then the background fabric to a sunny window; use the fabric pen to trace the design. Work Stem Stitches for the words.
2. Draw around various size coins on the wrong side of the fabric scraps; cut out circles. Filling in the tree shape, attach circles with French Knots, Straight Stitch stars, or buttons. Add buttons or French Knots in any empty areas. For the trunk, whipstitch a small fabric square to the tree bottom. Use a damp cotton swab to remove fabric pen markings. Insert the piece in the frame. ✽

Why not create a Signature Table Runner every year, until each member of your family has one? O Christmas Tree—how lovely are these button and fabric branches!

Woodland Felt Ornaments

• tissue paper • two 8" squares of felt for each ornament (tan for acorn and light teal for bird) • light green, dark green, teal, dark teal, and dark brown 3-ply Persian wool yarn • embroidery needle • pearl seed beads, beading thread, and a beading needle • polyester fiberfill • clear nylon thread

Refer to Embroidery Stitches, page 149, and Stitching Key, page 151, for embroidery stitches, yarn colors, and bead placement. Use 1 ply of yarn for all embroidery.

1. For either design, enlarge the pattern, page 151, to 200%. Trace onto tissue paper. Center and pin the pattern on one felt square. Follow the Stitching Key to embroider the design; carefully tear away the paper. Use beading thread to add beads.
2. Place the felt squares together; cut out shapes 1" beyond the design.
3. Matching the right sides and leaving an opening for turning, use a $1/2$" seam allowance to sew the shapes together. Trim the seam allowances to $1/4$". Clip the curves, turn right side out, and stuff with fiberfill; sew the opening closed.
4. For the hanger, knot 10" of clear thread at the top of the ornament. ❊

When you see Woodland Felt Ornaments nestled in a tree, you can almost hear the peaceful whisper of falling snow. Feeling festive? The redwork embroidery on the Cheers-to-You Towel is a high-spirited salute to the season.

Cheers-to-You Towel

- tissue paper • tea towel
- embroidery floss (we used dark red, red, and pink)
- embroidery needle

Refer to Embroidery Stitches, page 149, and Stitching Key, page 153, for embroidery stitches and floss colors. Use 3 strands of floss for all embroidery, except for ornament hangers (use 1 strand).
Enlarge the pattern, page 153, to 200%. Trace onto tissue paper. Center and pin the pattern on the towel bottom. Follow the Stitching Key to embroider the design; carefully tear away the paper. ✻

Olde World Santa

• foam scraps for arms and beard • 1½" dia. foam ball • 6" foam cone • craft knife • hot glue gun • scrap cardstock • Creative Paperclay® • medium-grit sandpaper • acrylic paint (white, brown, pink, tan, ivory, brown metallic, very dark brown, and green) • paintbrushes • transfer paper • disposable foam brush • craft glue • copper glitter • clear acrylic matte spray sealer

1. Enlarge the patterns, page 152, to 145%. Draw around the beard and arm patterns on the scrap foam. Cut the arms and beard from the foam, trimming each piece to about ³/₈" thick. Trim about ½" from the top of the cone. Hot glue the foam ball to the top of the cone. Make a small cone-shaped hat from cardstock and glue to the foam ball head. Glue the arms and the beard to the cone body (*Fig. 1*).

2. Cover the entire Santa with Paperclay, building the Paperclay into a softly rolled edge for the "fur" trim on the coat. Lightly build up the Paperclay for the eyebrows and nose. For the moustache, mittens, wreath, and wreath hanger, form each shape separately and then attach the shape to Santa (*Fig. 2*). Use the craft knife to add details and texture to the mittens, fur trim, eyebrows, moustache, beard, and wreath.

3. Once the Paperclay is **completely** dry, sand Santa until he is smooth. Paint Santa, shading the white areas with brown (*Fig. 3*).

4. Transfer the trim pattern to the bottom of Santa's coat. Paint the trim (*Fig. 4*).

5. Brush craft glue on fur, wreath hanger, berries, and coat trim motifs; sprinkle glitter on the wet glue. Working in a well-ventilated area, spray Santa with 2 coats of sealer. ❋

Fig. 3

Fig. 1

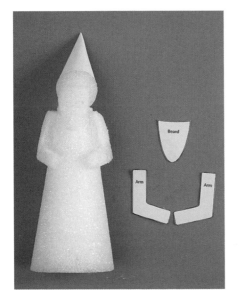

Fig. 2

Fig. 4

Historically, Santa has been depicted wearing almost every color imaginable, so you can choose any appealing hues for your Olde World Santa's robe.

Santa relies on the help of his trusted reindeer. That's why each figure of this Retro Reindeer family wears a little charm on a raffia collar—they're gifts of appreciation from Santa. So sweet!

Retro Reindeer

each small reindeer approx finished size:
 6" long x 3¹/₂" high (5" high to top of head)
each large reindeer approx finished size:
 8³/₄" long x 5" high (6¹/₄" high to top of head)
The large reindeer supplies and measurements are included in parentheses following the information for the small reindeer.

• aluminum foil • three (five) 2-oz. packages of modeling clay • 18-gauge wire • wire cutters • pliers • four 3¹/₂"-long (4¹/₂"-long) craft sticks • découpage glue • disposable foam brush • off-white handmade paper • dark brown and black acrylic paints and paintbrush • hot glue gun • 2 black seed beads • small charm • raffia

1. Referring to the Reindeer Table and **Fig. 1**, form pieces from crumpled foil and clay for the reindeer. For each antler, cut a 2" (3") and a 2½" (3½") wire length. Twist the wires together to form the antler. For the legs, trim 4 craft sticks to 2½" (4") long.

2. Wrap the flattened clay piece around the foil body and smooth the edges to cover the foil. Add the neck and head, smoothing the clay in place and shaping the head and neck into the desired position. Insert ½" of each leg into the body. Insert the antlers into the head (*Fig. 2*).

3. Cover the antlers and legs with clay. Shape a tail and 2 ears from clay and attach to the body. Add and smooth clay to shape the reindeer (*Fig. 3*).

4. Follow the manufacturer's instructions to bake the reindeer and the nose. Refer to **Fig. 4** and Découpaging, page 148, to cover the reindeer with torn pieces of handmade paper. (We used contrasting paper for our photo.)

5. Paint the hooves dark brown and nose black. Hot glue the bead eyes and the nose to the reindeer.

6. Thread the charm onto a raffia length and tie it around the reindeer's neck. ❊

Fig. 1

Fig. 2

Fig. 3

Fig. 4

PART	SHAPE	SMALL REINDEER	LARGE REINDEER
-	-	from crumpled foil	
body	cylinder	3¾"long x 1¼" dia.	5" long x 1½" dia.
-	-	from clay	
skin	flat	5" x 6"	7" x 7"
neck	drum	1" long x 1" dia.	1½"long x 1½" dia.
head	cone	2" long	2½" long
nose	heart	$5/16$" wide	$7/16$" wide

wraps, tags, & cards

Half the fun of giving a gift is in the presentation! These bags, tags, cards, boxes, and package toppers will finish your presents with a merry flair. Some, like the keepsake Frame Tags, are truly gifts in themselves!

Frame Tags

- frames (we used a magnetic acrylic frame and small wood frames) • scrapbook paper and cardstock • rub-on letters • dimensional stickers • acrylic paint • paintbrush • craft glue • circle, flower, and snowflake punches • buttons • embroidery floss • decorative brads • hot glue gun • sandpaper • painted chipboard letters • adhesive foam dots • crocheted mini Santa hat and mini pom-pom (found in the scrapbook store)

1. For the magnetic frame tag, personalize scrapbook paper with the rub-on letters and insert into the frame. Add a few dimensional stickers and attach to a wrapped package.
2. For the monogram frame tag, paint the wood frame edges. Cover the frame front with cardstock. Attach brads and floss-tied buttons to punched paper circles and flowers; glue to the frame. Add a rub-on monogram to a scrapbook paper piece; attach to the frame back. Decorate a gift box lid with scrapbook paper and a cardstock border. Hot glue the frame to the lid.
3. For the Santa hat frame tag, paint the frame; then, lightly sand. Insert scrapbook paper in the frame opening and add a chipboard letter name to the frame front with foam dots. Adhere punched cardstock snowflakes, the Santa hat, and mini pom-pom to the frame. ✷

If you're a papercraft enthusiast, why not gather your scraps and some dried naturals to create cards and gift wrap with an earth-friendly theme? You can also fashion package toppers with paper, yarn, felt or repurposed faux greenery.

Green Greetings

These special keepsake cards are easy to make with gathered bits from the craft room and garden. Decorate blank cards and envelopes with stamped or handwritten words, dried flowers and leaves, buttons, pages from an old dictionary, ribbon, and torn papers. Spell out "LOVE" with cinnamon sticks, raffia, dried apple slices, and string. Use foam dots to elevate parts of the card, such as the "Harmony" tag. Buttons form a joyous little tree. Natural elements line up on a gridded card and a ribbon border brings the seasonal message to the forefront of a word-lover's card. ❋

Naturally Nice

Wrap your gifts in simple, yet beautiful, handmade paper, or choose re-usable gift bags. Top with torn paper accents (add a heart cut from a dried bay leaf) and handmade gift tags. To make the tags, layer cardstock scraps and add stamped or handwritten words, paper rosettes, or even a cluster of pearls and beads. Attach the tags with ribbons or raffia. ❋

Berry Topper

Dress up a non-descript gift box with a scallop-edged cardstock piece, coordinating ribbon, a berry sprig, and a few glittery branches. Add a punch of color by gluing rickrack around the box sides. ❄

Snowflake Topper

• decorated round gift box
• cardstock • craft knife
• snowflake punch • craft glue • thick adhesive foam dots

1. Size the snowflake, page 155, to fit the gift box. Size another one, slightly smaller. (We enlarged the pattern to 167% and 122% for our 4" dia. box.) Use the enlarged patterns and a craft knife to cut cardstock snowflakes. Punch a small cardstock snowflake for the center. Cut a cardstock circle to fit the box top.
2. Glue the circle, then the large snowflake to the box top. Use foam dots to adhere the remaining snowflakes. ❄

Holly Leaf Take-Out Topper

• take-out style gift box • dark green and green felt • craft glue • red yarn • yarn needle

1. Enlarge the pattern, page 151, to 200%. Using the pattern, cut 4 felt leaves. Stack and glue 2 leaves together at the center; then, glue the stems together.
2. Cut an 8 yard yarn length. Wind a small ball at one end. Use the yarn needle to thread the loose end through the center of the ball. Make a second ball on the other end.
3. Wrap the yarn with the balls around the box and tie the leaves on top, winding the yarn around the stems several times. Glue the balls to the box. ❄

Photo Cards

• double-sided cardstock • photographs (or photocopied photos) • double-sided tape • ribbon • chipboard flowers and letters • decorative brad • adhesive foam dots

Cut a 10" x 7" cardstock piece. Matching the short ends, fold in half. (Use the card horizontally or vertically.) Trimming to fit, tape the photo to the card and add a cardstock mat if you'd like. Decorate the card as you wish—ribbon, chipboard elements, cardstock cutouts, and a brad all embellish our unique cards. ✳

Pop-Up Gift Card Holder

will hold a 3³⁄₈" x 2¹⁄₈" gift card
- ¹⁄₈ yard red silk fabric
- green silk fabric scrap • fusible interfacing • tracing paper • awl or craft knife • brass grommet with ¹⁄₄" dia. opening and setter • hammer • ³⁄₄ yd of ³⁄₈"w green velvet ribbon • gift card • ⁵⁄₈" square metal tag • fine point permanent marker • small jingle bells • fabric glue

1. Fuse interfacing to the back of the silk fabric pieces. Using the pattern, page 151, cut 2 holly leaves from green silk; set aside. Cut a 3³⁄₄" x 9" red piece. Press the short ends ¹⁄₄" to the wrong side twice.
2. Topstitch one pressed end. Pierce a small hole 1¹⁄₂" below the center of the finished end; set the grommet in the hole.
3. Match the wrong sides and pin one end of an 8" ribbon length under the remaining pressed end of the fabric piece (*Fig. 1*); topstitch the pressed end, catching the ribbon in the stitching.

4. Press the side edges ¹⁄₄" to the wrong side; matching the wrong sides and short ends, fold the piece in half and topstitch along the side and bottom edges, being careful not to catch the ribbon. Pull the ribbon end through the grommet. Place the gift card in the holder (this will draw the ribbon inside). Write "Pull" on the tag. Trimming the ribbon as desired, sew the tag to the ribbon end.
5. Sew the bells and leaves to the front of the card holder. Glue two 9" ribbon lengths back-to-back and glue the ends to the back of the holder for the handle. ❊

Fig. 1

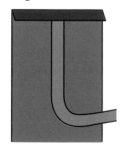

What's the best gift for loved ones who can't come home for Christmas? A greeting card featuring the smiles of everyone they're missing! If Santa's delivering a gift card, make it special with a fabric card holder.

Pom-Pom Bow

shown on center back package
approx size: 6" dia.

• 2³/₄ yards of 1¹/₂"w wire-edged ribbon (bow and streamers only)

1. For streamers, cut a 27" ribbon length and set aside.
2. Referring to **Figs. 1-2**, loop the remaining ribbon and cut notches at the center, leaving at least ¹/₄" between the notch points.
3. Tie the streamer ribbon around the bow center at the notches. Starting with the innermost layer, pull the loops out and toward the bow center *(Fig. 3)*. Twist and shape the loops into a full bow. Trim all ribbon ends. ❋

Fig. 1

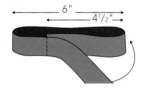

Fig. 2

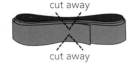

Fig. 3

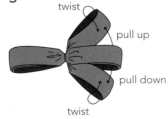

Loopy Bow

shown on left package
approx size: 6" dia.

• 1 yard each of 1¹/₂"w and ³/₈"w ribbon • hot glue gun • 1" dia. button

Cut six 12" ribbon lengths. Hot glue the ends of each ribbon length together, forming a loop. Hot glue the loops together in a circle and top off with a button center. ❋

Layered Loop Bow

shown on right package
approx size: 5¹/₂" long

• 1 yard of 1¹/₂"w double-faced ribbon (bow only) • double-sided tape or a small stapler

Referring to **Figs. 4-6**, loop ribbon back and forth in a figure-eight motion, taping at the center before making each new loop; make 2 sets of loops and a small round center loop. Or, you can staple all the loops together through the hole in the center loop at the end. ❋

Fig. 4

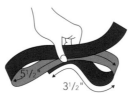

Fig. 5

Fig. 6

Purchased gift wrap just doesn't have the special look of handmade bows and boxes. You'll be surprised to learn how easy it is to loop and fold these elegant presentations.

Origami Boxes
• heavy cardstock • scrapbook paper • spray adhesive • craft knife • bone folder or stylus • assorted embellishments (we used tissue paper, assorted ribbons and tags, beaded wire, and stickers)

Always work in a well-ventilated area when using spray adhesive.

1. For the small box, cut a 6" square each from cardstock and scrapbook paper. Adhere the paper to one side of the cardstock.
2. Referring to **Fig. 1**, use a ruler to divide the piece into nine equal squares; lightly mark the squares on the cardstock side.
3. Use the craft knife to cut away the corner squares. To create the box depth, refer to **Fig. 2** and lightly mark a line ¹/₄" away from the center lines on each side. Use the bone folder and a ruler to score these lines.
4. For the flaps, cut from the depth line to the opposite corner (*Fig. 3*); discard the cut-away triangles.
5. Wrap the gift in tissue paper and place in the box center. Refer to **Fig. 4** to fold three flaps along the scored lines. Tuck the fourth flap under the folded flaps to secure the box. Add a tag, ribbon, beaded wire bow, or other embellishment.
6. For the medium box, repeat Steps 1-5 using a 9" square and ³/₄" depth.
7. For the large box, repeat Steps 1-5 using a 12" square and 1" depth. ✽

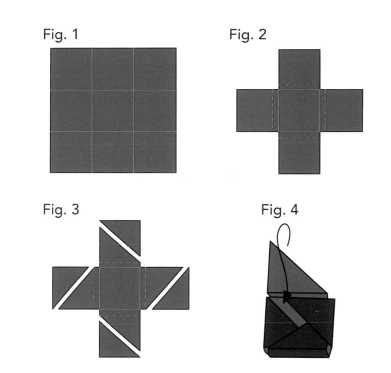

Fig. 1   Fig. 2

Fig. 3   Fig. 4

Photo Tags

- cardstock • circle and square punches • scrapbook paper • craft glue • small hole punch • photograph (or photocopied photo)
- alphabet dies and die-cutting tool • double-sided tape • rub-on letters
- ribbons and trims

1. For each tag, cut a 4$\frac{1}{4}$" x 6$\frac{1}{8}$" cardstock piece and trim the corners. Punch a scrapbook paper circle or square and glue to the tag top. Punch a small hole through both layers for the ribbon.

2. Trim the photo to fit the tag. Die-cut the first letter of the recipient's name from the photo. (Don't throw away the cut-away bits yet. You may need to glue some of them in place on the cardstock, like the tops around the "m.")

3. Tape the photo to the tag, gluing any small pieces in place. Add the remaining letters with rub-ons.

4. Add ribbons and trims to the tag. ❋

Tree Bag

finished size: 9"w x 10¹/₄"h
- ³/₈ yard wool felt • wool felt scraps (white, green, and gold) • embroidery floss (red, white, gold, and green)
- fabric glue • 10 mm white pom-poms
- flat red sequins • beading needle
- white seed beads

For all sewing, match the right sides and raw edges and use a ¹/₂" seam allowance. Use 2 strands of floss for all Embroidery Stitches, page 149.

1. Cut a 10" x 26" red felt piece. Fold the short ends 1" to the wrong side; topstitch along the raw edges and folds.
2. Matching the short ends, fold the felt in half and sew the side seams. Flatten and center each side seam against the bottom of the bag; sew across each corner 1³/₄" from the point *(Fig. 1)*. Turn the bag right side out.
3. For each handle, cut two 1" x 12" red felt strips; stack and topstitch along the long edges. Sew the handle ends to the inside at the top of the bag.
4. Enlarge the patterns, page 153, to 153%. Using the patterns, cut the tree, ornaments, and star from felt scraps. Work floss Running Stitches to sew the tree and star appliqués to the bag front.
5. Glue the ornaments and pom-poms to the tree. Attach a sequin to each ornament with a French Knot. Sew the beads to the tree. ❋

Fig. 1

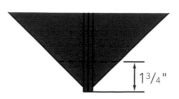

1³/₄"

Photo gift tags like these are every bit as nice as the gifts they accompany. The same is true of a wool felt bag—it can be reused and enjoyed for many Christmases to come.

These distinctive wraps will convey your best wishes for the happiest of holidays!

Velvet Gift Bag

approx finished size: 8"w x 15"h
- 5/8 yard fabric • ribbon • holiday brooch

Cut a 17" x 20" fabric piece. Matching the right sides and long edges and using a 1/2" seam allowance, sew the piece into a tube; finger press the seam allowances open. Centering the seam on the back, sew across the bottom of the bag. Turn the top edge 1/2", then 4" to the wrong side and hem. Turn the bag right side out. Place the gift in the bag and tie with ribbon. Attach a pretty brooch for 2 gifts in one. ❋

Fabric-covered Box

- papier-mâché box (any size or shape) • fabrics to cover box and lid • spray adhesive • fabric glue
- ribbons • scrapbook paper • rub-on letters
- mini copper frame

Always work in a well-ventilated area when using spray adhesive.

1. Measure around the box; add 1". Measure the height of the box; add 2". Cut a fabric piece the determined measurements. Spray the box with adhesive. Wrap the fabric piece around the box, centering the fabric on the box and overlapping the ends at back. Turn the raw end 1/2" to the wrong side and glue. Clipping as necessary, fold and glue the edges to the bottom and inside.
2. Draw around the box lid on the wrong side of the fabric. Cut the fabric 1" beyond the drawn line(s). Spray the lid with adhesive. Press the fabric onto the lid, clipping the fabric as necessary to wrap to the sides. Glue a piece of ribbon to the lid sides, covering the fabric raw edges.
3. Place the gift in the box. Tie ribbons around the box (we used 3 coordinating colors) and add rub-ons to a scrapbook paper tag inserted in a mini copper frame. ❋

Fabric Pouch

approx finished size: 11 1/2"w x 9"h
- 3/4 yard fabric • 1 1/2 yards of 1"w grosgrain ribbon • mini wreath

When sewing, always match right sides and raw edges and use a 1/2" seam allowance.

1. Cut a 12 1/2" x 26" fabric piece. Trim 2 corners (*Fig. 1*).
2. Press the bottom edge 1/4" to the wrong side twice; hem.
3. Fold the bottom up 9". Sew the side seams. Turn the pouch right side out.
4. Press the remaining raw edges 1/4" to the wrong side twice; hem.
5. Fold 1 ribbon end 17" toward the center. Place the folded end on the flap front (leaving about a 1 1/4" loop pointing toward the flap); sew the ribbon in place (*Fig. 2*).
6. Place the gift in the pouch, slip the shorter ribbon end through the wreath, wrap the longer end around the pouch and through the loop; tie a bow. ❋

Fig. 1   Fig. 2

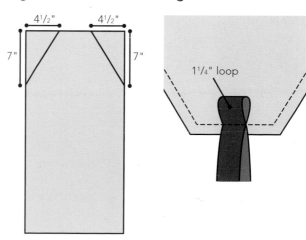

Gift Card Holders
each will hold a 3³/₈" x 2¹/₈"
gift card

For each gift card holder, enlarge the desired pattern, page 158, to 200%. Using the pattern, cut the holder from cardstock. Use a bone folder to score the holder as shown by the dashed lines on the pattern.

Highlight sections of the holder by cutting scrapbook paper overlays. Glue the overlays in place. Use a glue pen and glitter to accent the holder and cardstock cut-outs.

Fold the gift card holder along the scored lines and glue close to the edges to secure. Place the gift card inside and embellish with ribbons and cut-outs. A star charm makes the gift even more special. ❊

Glittery Tags

• scrapbook paper and double-sided cardstock • circle and hole punches • scallop-edged scissors • craft glue • glitter • embellishments (vintage postage stamps, dimensional stickers, chipboard letters, brads, felt borders, and a key) • ribbons • buttons • double-sided tape

1. For the round tag, layer and glue punched and scalloped scrapbook paper circles. Add glitter accents. Embellish as desired. Knot ribbons and a button through a small hole.
2. For the folded tag, cut a piece of cardstock 1¹/₂ times longer than the finished tag. Fold the top to the front at the finished length. Cut an opening in the flap a bit larger than a dimensional sticker. Adhere the sticker and secure the folded flap with corner brads and a key. Embellish as desired. Thread ribbon through the fold and knot a button at the center.
3. For the snowflake tag, layer and glue ribbon and borders to a cardstock tag. Add glitter accents. Embellish as desired. Knot ribbons and a button through a small hole. ❊

Glittery tags or gift
card holders add
special flair to that
perfect present!

❄ christmas keepsakes ❄

*Some gifts are just for fun. Others are chosen for their practical nature.
And then there are keepsakes like these! An audio recording of a
child's bedtime story, a whimsical ceramic plate, a box to hold Christmas
wishes—each will be cherished and enjoyed for a lifetime.*

Story Time CD or DVD

• child's favorite Christmas storybook • double-sided tape • scrapbook paper and cardstock • craft glue • assorted ribbons • CD or DVD (recorded with story read by Grandma) • rub-on letters • glitter

1. Line the inside front cover and first page of the book with scrapbook paper. Cut a coordinating scrapbook paper pocket for the recorded disc. Trim the pocket edges with ribbon. Glue the pocket to the book along the top, bottom, and left side. Place the disc in the pocket.

2. Cut 2 ribbon lengths to go around the book, plus 1/2"; sew the lengths together along the long edges. Wrap the ribbon band around the book, overlapping the ends at the front; glue the ends together.

3. Enlarge the label pattern, page 158, to 146%; using the pattern, cut a cardstock label. Add rub-on letters and glitter the label edges. Glue the label to the ribbon band. ❄

Snowman Plate

Begin a tradition of going to a do-it-yourself pottery studio to create a new keepsake each year.

• sized pattern (page 158) • graphite transfer paper • ballpoint pen
• plate and paints supplied by the pottery studio

Follow Sizing Patterns, page 148, to enlarge the pattern, page 158, to fit your plate. (We enlarged the pattern to 268% to fit our 12" square plate.) Take the pattern and a piece of graphite transfer paper to the studio. Wipe the plate with a damp sponge to remove any dust. Use the ballpoint pen to transfer the pattern to the plate (the lines will disappear when it's fired). Leaving white areas unpainted, basecoat the background with several coats of blue to intensify the color. Paint the design details, again using several coats. Leave the plate at the shop to be fired. ❄

St. Nick's Wish Box

• 8¹/₂"w x 5¹/₄"d x 3¹/₂"h wooden box • wood putty • wood glue • four wood knobs for feet • handsaw • decorative wood trim • sandpaper • tack cloth • acrylic paints and paintbrushes • graphite transfer paper • black fine-point permanent pen • clear acrylic matte spray sealer • fabric glue • soft thick fabrics to line box • yarn

1. Remove the latch hardware and fill any holes with putty. Glue wood knobs to the bottom of the box. Cut the trim to fit, mitering at the corners. Glue the trim to the lid and box. Fill in the corners with putty. Sand the box and wipe it with a tack cloth to remove the dust.

2. Basecoat the box inside and out. Enlarge the patterns, page 154, to 154% and transfer them to the box. Paint the designs and add details with the pen. Sand the box lightly and apply sealer in a well-ventilated area.

3. Line the inside lid and bottom of the box with fabric. (We used pieces cut from old sweaters for a cozy lining.) Finish it off with yarn glued around the fabric edges. ❄

Give a smile for Christmas this year! The Snowman Plate will serve up a happy dish of cookies or other holiday treats, while St. Nick's Wish Box magically conveys to Santa the contents of any letter a child places inside.

❄ pampered pets ❄

Those trusting eyes and furry faces—pets amuse us with their antics and melt our hearts with their affection. Maybe that's why so many of us think of our dogs and cats as family members. For Sparky, why not make a Dog Coat of fleece fabric? He'll love its warmth almost as much as the attention it will bring.

Pet Stockings

Shown on page 56
- felt • pinking shears • fabric glue
- embroidery floss • cardboard
- yarn

1. Enlarge the patterns, page 152, to 200%. Cut one stocking from felt. Pin this stocking on another piece of felt; stitch about 1/2" from the side and bottom edges of the stocking, leaving the top open. Trim around the stocking with the pinking shears. Sew a 5" x 1" folded strip of pinked felt to the inside stocking back for a hanger.
2. Cut a dog or cat silhouette from felt and glue to the stocking. Add floss details.
3. Make a few pom-poms, page 149, and sew them to the stocking with yarn (we made 1³/₄", 2", and 2¹/₂" pom-poms). ❄

Dog Coat

- fleece • removable fabric marking pen • hook and loop fasteners

1. Refer to Sizing Patterns, page 148, and enlarge or reduce the pattern, page 157, to fit your dog, making length adjustments as necessary. Use the pattern to cut the coat from fleece. Use the fabric marking pen to mark strap placement lines.
2. Drape the coat over your dog and measure across his belly from one strap mark on the coat to the other; add 3". Cut a 5" wide strap the determined measurement.
3. Matching the right sides and long edges, fold the strap piece and use a 1/2" seam allowance to sew across one end and along the long raw edge. Turn the strap right side out and topstitch all the edges.
4. Press the raw edges of the coat 1/2" to the wrong side; topstitch. Matching the pattern markings, sew the raw end of the strap to one of the strap markings on the coat inside.
5. Sew a hook and loop fastener to the loose strap end and on the coat right side at the strap marking. Sew another fastener at the front neck closure. ❄

Quick to make and fun to fill with Christmas surprises, Pet Stockings (page 54) will please the four-pawed people in your home. For the world's best pup, how about a tail-wagging bag of homemade Doggie Treats?

Doggie Treats

2 cups whole-wheat flour
1 cup all-purpose flour
1 cup yellow cornmeal
1/2 cup nonfat dry milk powder
1/2 teaspoon garlic powder
1 package (3 ounces) beef jerky dog treats, finely chopped
1/2 cup shredded Cheddar cheese
2/3 cup vegetable oil
3/4 cup beef or chicken broth
2 eggs

In a mixing bowl, combine flours, cornmeal, dry milk, and garlic powder. Stir in beef pieces and cheese. Add oil, broth, and eggs; stir until well blended.

On a lightly floured surface, pat dough to 3/8" thickness. Use a 1 7/8" x 3 5/8" bone-shaped cookie cutter to cut out treats. Transfer to an ungreased baking sheet. Bake in a preheated 300° oven for 20 to 22 minutes or until firm and bottoms are lightly browned. Transfer treats to a wire rack to cool. Store in an airtight container in the refrigerator. **Yield:** about 2 dozen dog treats

Doggie Treats Gift Bag

• black and brown cardstock • craft glue stick • medium-size brown paper bag • hot glue gun • natural raffia • bagged Doggie Treats and copy of recipe • hole punch • jute twine • bone-shaped cookie cutter

1. Enlarge the patterns, page 156, to 205%. Cut dogs and small bones from black cardstock and a large bone from brown cardstock.
2. Use the glue stick to adhere the dogs to the bag. Hot glue a raffia bow to the bag; trim with the small bones. Place the treats and recipe in the bag and hot glue the bag closed.
3. Punch a hole near the bag top and tie the cookie cutter to the bag with twine. Write "Doggie Treats" on the large bone and layer it on a piece of black cardstock. Trim close to the edge and glue to the bag. ❋

❄ *a flurry of fast gifts* ❄

It's simple to create heartwarming gifts that won't break your budget. Many of these ideas, such as the Ornament Vase and Pretty Poinsettia Mini Bags, are also a snap to create in multiples, making them perfect for party favors and co-worker gifts!

Ornament Vase

• ball ornament • craft glue • napkin ring • rub-on design • fresh flowers

After removing the hanger hardware, glue the ornament to the napkin ring and apply the rub-on design. Now fill the ornament with water and insert flowers for a lovely little gift vase. ❋

Pretty Poinsettia Mini Bags

For each bag:
• 4$\frac{1}{2}$" x 14" fabric piece • 1$\frac{1}{3}$ yds of $\frac{3}{4}$"w grosgrain ribbon

For all sewing, match the right sides and use a $\frac{1}{4}$" seam allowance.

1. For each bag, match the short ends and fold the rectangle in half. Sew along the side edges; turn right side out. Press the top edge of the fabric $\frac{1}{4}$" to the wrong side twice; hem.

2. To make the poinsettia, cut eighteen 2" ribbon lengths. Cut each length into a petal shape. Thread the petals together, pinching and folding each petal point as you string it on *(Fig. 1)*. Once all petals are strung, tightly tie the thread ends together, forming the poinsettia. Adjust the petals as necessary. Sew the flower to the remaining ribbon length, and tie it around the fabric bag after inserting the gift. ❋

Fig. 1

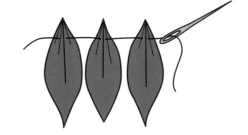

Glass Ice Bucket Candle

Center a pillar candle in a vintage glass ice bucket and surround it with fresh seasonal cranberries. ❋

Never leave a burning candle unattended.

Merry Mini Stockings
Makes 10 stockings

• ⅓ yd of 54"w ecru felt • felt scraps in assorted colors • embroidery floss • small buttons • fabric glue • candy canes

1. Enlarge the patterns, page 153, to 131%. For each stocking, use the patterns and cut 2 stockings (1 in reverse), a cuff, flowers, and 2 leaves from felt.
2. Place the stocking pieces wrong sides together and use 3 strands of floss to work Blanket Stitches, page 149, along the side and bottom edges.
3. Sew a button to the center of the daisy. Attach the posy center to the posy with Blanket Stitches. Glue the leaves, flowers, and cuff to the stocking.
4. For the hanger, glue the ends of a small felt strip to the inside back of the stocking top. Place a candy cane in the stocking. ❋

Snowman Slippers

- pair of slippers • white, orange, and black felt
- embroidery floss • snowflake buttons

1. Enlarge the patterns, page 154, to 164%. Using the patterns, cut appliqués from felt.
2. Using 3 strands of floss, whipstitch the appliqués to the slippers. Sew the buttons to the slippers. ✳

Create elegance in an instant with a Glass Ice Bucket Candle. Want to fashion presents for just pennies? You can with Merry Mini Stockings! Fun Snowman Slippers will warm toes—and hearts—with your thoughtfulness.

Beribboned Ornament

- 3½" dia. glass ornament • craft knife • assorted ribbons/ trims • hot glue gun • 1¼" dia. jingle bell • ¾" dia. flat bead • numeral stickers • cream cardstock • 2 self-adhesive clear tags • liquid fray preventative

To celebrate a memorable year in a loved one's life, make a Beribboned Ornament in just minutes.

1. Remove the cap from the ornament. Use the craft knife to enlarge the bottom opening in the cap; set aside.
2. Cut five 20" lengths of assorted ribbons/trims. Set aside one ribbon length.
3. Crisscrossing at the center bottom and spacing evenly around the ornament, glue 4 ribbon/trim lengths to the ornament. Do not trim excess ribbon/trim.
4. Thread a jingle bell onto the reserved ribbon length; thread both ends through the bead. With the ribbon ends apart, glue the bead to the ornament center bottom. Wrap and glue the ribbon around the ornament.
5. Thread the loose ribbon ends through the cap opening and replace the cap on the ornament.
6. Adhere stickers to cardstock and cut out. Sandwich the year between the tags. Knot a length of ribbon through a hole in the layered tag and tie the ends around the ornament neck.
7. For the hanger, thread a ribbon length through the wire loop and knot the ends together. Apply liquid fray preventative to all ribbon/ trim ends. ❈

creating fun *food gifts* for the HOLIDAYS

Snacks, mixes, *cookies*, a casserole—there are nearly two dozen yummy recipes here to please every *lucky* recipient. We show you how to make each gift look as *good* as it tastes!

❄ food gifts ❄

Gifts from the kitchen are always welcome! The savory seasonings in Garden Herb Bread Blend turn an ordinary hot roll mix into fragrant loaves of bread. Your favorite baker will appreciate the bread board and festive spice packet.

Garden Herb Bread Blend

- 1/3 cup dried parsley flakes
- 1/3 cup dried minced onions
- 2 1/2 tablespoons dried basil
- 2 1/2 teaspoons dried thyme
- 2 1/2 teaspoons dried oregano
- 1 1/4 teaspoons garlic powder

Blend herbs together in bowl. Package in airtight container or bag.

Yield: 1 cup (enough for 6 loaves of bread)

Bread Recipe

- 3 to 4 teaspoons Garden Herb Bread Blend
- 1 package hot roll mix
- 4 tablespoons butter, divided
- 1 egg

Add Garden Herb Bread Blend to dry hot roll mix. Follow instructions on hot roll mix package for mixing, kneading, and resting. Shape dough into regular-size or mini loaves or follow instructions on package for rolls. Allow dough to rise. Bake regular-size bread loaves in greased loaf pans in a preheated 375° oven for 35 to 40 minutes. Bake mini loaves about 10 minutes less, 25 to 30 minutes. Brush tops with remaining 2 tablespoons butter.

Bread Board

Enlarge the label, page 157, to 160% and photocopy onto cardstock; color with pencils and embellish with glitter. Glue the label on a tag trimmed with ribbons and a decorative brad. Decorate a paper sack with a pinked cardstock square and the label. Place a bag of Garden Herb Bread Blend inside (along with a copy of the Bread recipe) and tie the sack to a bread board with ribbon. ❋

garden herb
bread blend

Spiced Cider Mix

Include a bag of cinnamon candies to complete this special treat.

1 cup orange breakfast drink mix
1 cup sugar
$1/2$ cup instant tea
1 package (4 ounces) sweetened lemonade drink mix
$1/2$ teaspoon ground cinnamon
$1/4$ teaspoon ground cloves
$1/4$ teaspoon ground allspice

Combine orange breakfast drink mix and remaining ingredients in a large bowl, stirring well. Store in an airtight container. Mix can be frozen up to 1 month. Give with serving instructions. **Yield:** about 3 cups mix

Serving Instructions:
Combine 3 tablespoons Spiced Cider Mix, 1 teaspoon cinnamon candies, and 1 cup boiling water. Stir well.

Wrapped Mug

• mug • brown, cream, and gold cardstock • striped vellum • scallop-edged scissors • craft glue • hole punch, eyelets, and setter • ribbons • scrapbook paper • large needle • alphabet stamp set • ink pad • linen thread • adhesive foam dots • dimensional snowman sticker • bagged Spiced Cider Mix and cinnamon candies

1. For the sleeve, tear a piece of brown cardstock to fit around the mug plus $1/2$". Layer and glue cream cardstock and vellum on the brown cardstock, scalloping and trimming the edges as you wish. Referring to **Fig. 1**, trim the corners from the sleeve and attach the eyelets. Overlapping the tabs under the handle, wrap the sleeve around the mug and tie a ribbon bow through the eyelets.

2. For the label, layer and glue torn and cut pieces of paper and gold cardstock. Pierce holes around the outer edges and stamp "SPICED CIDER" on the label. Attach an eyelet to one end of the label and knot linen thread through the eyelet. Use foam dots to attach the snowman to the label; then, attach the label to the sleeve. Add bagged mix and candies and give with serving instructions. ❋

Fig. 1

With its colorfully wrapped mug and holiday flavor, Spiced Cider Mix will warm the heart of someone special. Help a friend serve a Christmas feast by supplying an Apple-Cheese Torte on a ribbon-embellished stand.

Apple-Cheese Torte

Crust

- 1 cup butter
- $^2/_3$ cup sugar
- $^1/_2$ teaspoon vanilla extract
- 2 cups all-purpose flour

Filling

- 4 Granny Smith apples, cored, peeled, and thinly sliced (6 cups)
- $^3/_4$ cup sugar, divided
- 1 teaspoon ground cinnamon
- 2 teaspoons lemon juice
- 1 package (8 ounces) cream cheese, softened
- 2 teaspoons vanilla extract
- 2 eggs
- $^1/_4$ cup sliced almonds

For crust, cream butter and sugar until smooth. Add vanilla and flour, blending well. Press crust mixture into bottom and $^3/_4$ up sides of a 10" springform pan.

For filling, combine apples with $^1/_2$ cup sugar, cinnamon, and lemon juice. Mix well and set aside. Beat cream cheese, remaining $^1/_4$ cup sugar, vanilla, and eggs. Pour over crust. Pour apple mixture over cream cheese mixture.

Bake in a preheated 450° oven for 10 minutes, then at 400° for 25 to 35 minutes or until top is golden brown. Allow to cool and remove sides of pan. Sprinkle with sliced almonds.

Yield: one 10" torte

Contributed by Ron Werle

Torte Stand

Cut 3 ribbon lengths long enough to drape over your cake stand with the ends about $^3/_4$" above the table. Use double-sided tape to tape the ends of each ribbon length to the wrong side to form a point. Sew a jingle bell to each point. Center and glue a narrow ribbon on each ribbon length. Arrange the ribbons and some greenery sprigs on the cake stand and place the Apple-Cheese Torte on top. ✱

Crazy Mixed-Up Popcorn

- 6 cups popped popcorn
- 3 cups crisp rice cereal squares
- 2 cups toasted oat O-shaped cereal
- 1½ cups dry roasted peanuts
- 1 cup pecan halves
- 1 cup firmly packed brown sugar
- ½ cup butter or margarine
- ¼ cup light corn syrup
- 1 teaspoon vanilla extract
- ¼ teaspoon baking soda

Stir together first 5 ingredients in a lightly greased roasting pan.

Bring brown sugar, butter, and corn syrup to a boil in a 3-quart saucepan over medium heat, stirring constantly. Boil sugar mixture, without stirring, 5 minutes or until a candy thermometer registers 250°. Remove from heat; stir in vanilla and baking soda.

Pour over popcorn mixture and stir until coated.

Bake in a preheated 250° oven for 1 hour, stirring every 20 minutes. Cool in pan on a wire rack; break apart. Store in an airtight container.

Yield: about 14 cups popcorn

Popcorn Tin

- bagged Crazy Mixed-Up Popcorn • lidded container
- cardstock • scallop-edged scissors • double-sided tape
- gold chalk • adhesive foam dots • alphabet stamps • ink pad • ribbons • hole punch

1. Place bagged popcorn in the container. For the label, layer cardstock circles, scalloping the edges of the top and bottom circles.

2. Enlarge the patterns, page 157, to 144%. Using the patterns, cut cardstock "popcorn" pieces. Chalk the edges; adhere to the label with tape and foam dots. Stamp "Crazy Mixed-Up Popcorn" on the label. Tie ribbon around the container and attach the label with foam dots.

3. Cut and layer a cardstock tag, scalloping one end. Adhere a popcorn piece to the tag and personalize. Thread ribbon through a punched hole and tie to the container. ❋

Snackers will go mad for a tin of Crazy Mixed-Up Popcorn. Know someone who's wild about chocolate? A Triple Chocolate Chip Cookie with a bottled mocha drink is sure to hit the spot.

Triple Chocolate Chip Cookies

1 package (16 ounces) refrigerated chocolate chip cookie dough
1 cup white chocolate chips
1 cup milk chocolate chips
1 teaspoon vanilla extract

Combine all ingredients and mix well. Drop by tablespoonfuls onto ungreased baking sheets. Bake in a preheated 350° oven for 12 to 15 minutes.
Yield: about 2 dozen cookies

Cookie Holder

• double-sided cardstock
• double-sided tape • rub-on letters • 1³/₈" and ¹/₈" circle punches • ribbon • bottled coffee drinks • individually wrapped Triple Chocolate Chip Cookies

Enlarge the patterns on page 157 to 142%. For each holder, use the patterns and cut a cardstock cookie holder and scallop-edged valance. Discard the cookie window and bottle opening pieces. Fold on the dashed lines. Tape the flap to the holder along the top fold line. Tape the valance to the holder above the window.
Add a rub-on name to a punched tag and tie it to the holder with ribbon. Tape a punched circle to the bottle lid and slip the cookie holder over the neck. Insert a cookie in the holder. ✳

food gifts ✳ **69**

Pumpkin-Apple Butter

- 2 cans (15 ounces each) canned pumpkin
- 2 cups peeled, cored, and shredded Granny Smith apples
- 2 cups no-sugar-added apple juice
- 1 cup firmly packed brown sugar
- 2 teaspoons ground cinnamon
- 1 teaspoon ground ginger
- 1/2 teaspoon ground cloves
- 1/4 teaspoon salt

Combine all ingredients in a 4-quart slow cooker. Cook on HIGH for 5 hours, stirring every 2 hours. Store in a covered container in the refrigerator for up to 2 months.
Yield: about 5½ cups pumpkin-apple butter

Two great flavors of the season meld into an unforgettable spread in Pumpkin-Apple Butter. Surprise someone with a basket of crackers and an Apricot Cheese Log made with tastebud-tingling apricot brandy and sharp Cheddar cheese.

Beaded Jars

• 4-ounce jelly jars • Pumpkin-Apple Butter • metal spray primer and black metal spray paint • medium- and fine-gauge wire • wire cutters • glass beads • double-sided tape • scrapbook paper and cardstock

Prime, then paint each ring and lid in a well-ventilated area and let dry. Fill each jar and secure the lid. Leaving a 2" tail, wrap medium-gauge wire around the jar just below the lid. Twist the wire around itself and form a handle loop by attaching the wire to the opposite side. Curl the wire ends. String beads on fine-gauge wire and wrap it around the handle. Tape a scrapbook paper circle to the lid and a computer-printed cardstock label to the front of the jar. ❄

Apricot Cheese Log

1/2	cup finely chopped dried apricots
5	tablespoons apricot brandy
2	cups (8 ounces) shredded sharp Cheddar cheese
4	ounces cream cheese, softened
1/8	teaspoon dry mustard
3/4	cup slivered almonds, toasted and coarsely chopped
	Crackers to serve

In a small bowl, combine apricots and brandy. Cover and let stand 1 hour.

In a medium bowl, combine Cheddar cheese, cream cheese, and dry mustard; beat about 3 minutes or until fluffy. Stir in apricot mixture. Cover and chill 1 hour.

Place cheese mixture on plastic wrap; shape into an 8" long roll. Press almonds into cheese roll. Wrap in plastic wrap. Store in refrigerator. Serve with crackers.

Yield: 1 cheese log (about 1 3/4 cups cheese)

Gift Basket

• basket • cardstock and scrapbook paper • scallop-edged scissors • double-sided tape • seasonal greeting stamp • ink pad • hole punch • ribbons • fabric for basket liner • wrapped Apricot Cheese Log and crackers

1. For the tag, layer cardstock and scrapbook paper circles, scalloping the edge of the bottom circle. Stamp the top circle and punch a hole near the tag top. Thread a ribbon length through the hole, around the basket handle, and back through the hole. Trim the ribbon ends long enough to hang below the tag at the bottom and tape in place. Tie a multi-loop bow around the basket handle.
2. Line the basket with fabric. Tie bows around the cheese log and crackers and place them in the basket. ❆

Caramel Sauce with Gingerbread Spoons

These edible spoons are delicious served with ice cream and Caramel Sauce.

Caramel Sauce

- ½ cup butter or margarine
- 1¼ cups firmly packed brown sugar
- 2 tablespoons light corn syrup
- ½ cup whipping cream

Gingerbread Spoons

- ½ cup butter or margarine, softened
- ¾ cup firmly packed dark brown sugar
- 1 large egg
- ⅓ cup molasses
- 2½ tablespoons lemon juice
- 3 to 3½ cups all-purpose flour, divided
- 1 tablespoon baking powder
- ¼ teaspoon baking soda
  Dash of salt
- 1½ teaspoons ground ginger
- 1 teaspoon ground cinnamon
- ¼ teaspoon ground cloves

For caramel sauce, melt butter in a small heavy saucepan over low heat; add brown sugar and corn syrup. Bring to a boil; cook, stirring constantly, 1 minute or until sugar dissolves. Gradually add cream; return to a boil. Cool completely. Give with gingerbread spoons.

For gingerbread spoons, beat butter at medium speed with an electric mixer until creamy; gradually add brown sugar, beating well. Add egg, molasses, and lemon juice; beat well.

Combine 1 cup flour and next 6 ingredients; stir well. Add to butter mixture, beating until blended. Gradually add enough remaining flour to make a stiff dough. Cover and chill dough 1 hour.

Divide dough into 2 portions. Roll each portion on a lightly greased cookie sheet to ¼" thickness; cover and freeze until firm.

Using a standard tablespoon as a pattern, cut spoons from dough with a sharp knife, about 2" apart. Remove excess dough from cookie sheet.

Repeat procedure with remaining frozen dough. Combine scraps of dough and repeat procedure until all dough is used.

Bake in a preheated 350° oven for 10 minutes or until golden. Let cool 1 minute on cookie sheets. Remove to wire racks; let cookies cool completely.

Yield: about 2 cups sauce and 3½ dozen spoons

Caramel Sauce Jar

- lidded glass jar filled with Caramel Sauce • light green, blue, and white cardstock
- snowflake and small and medium circle punches • craft glue • coarse iridescent glitter • black fine-point permanent pen • Gingerbread Spoons • cello bags • ribbon

1. For the sleeve, cut a piece of light green cardstock to fit around the jar plus 1". Cut a blue cardstock piece slightly smaller. Use the circle punches to punch a snowman from the blue cardstock piece; discard punched out pieces. Punch snowflakes from white cardstock. Layer and glue the blue and green cardstock pieces together.

2. For snow, tear one long edge of a 1"w white cardstock strip the length of the blue piece. Glue the snow and snowflakes to the sleeve. Apply glitter as desired. Draw the snowman details and add a seasonal message. Overlapping the edges, glue the sleeve around the jar.

3. Place each Gingerbread Spoon in a cello bag. Tie a ribbon and several bagged spoons around the jar lid. ❊

Want to be sweet to an ice cream fan? Caramel Sauce with Gingerbread Spoons will make a favorite frozen dessert even more fun to eat.

food gifts ❄ *73*

Double Chocolate Cupcakes

1 package (18.25 ounces) chocolate cake mix and ingredients needed to make cake
1 cup mini semi-sweet chocolate chips
1 cup white chocolate chips
2 tablespoons butter
2 cups confectioners sugar
3 to 4 tablespoons half and half
1/2 teaspoon vanilla extract
White coarse decorating sugar

In a bowl, combine cake mix and necessary ingredients. Beat at low speed for 30 seconds. Beat at medium speed for 2 minutes. Stir in mini chocolate chips. Line muffin pans with aluminum foil baking cups; fill cups 3/4 full. Bake in a preheated 350° oven for 15 to 18 minutes or until a toothpick inserted in center comes out clean. Remove from pans and cool on wire racks.

For frosting, place white chocolate chips and butter in a microwave-safe bowl. Microwave on MEDIUM until chocolate softens, stirring frequently until smooth; allow to cool. Beat in confectioners sugar, half and half, and vanilla until smooth.

Spoon frosting into a decorating bag fitted with a large round tip. Pipe frosting onto each cupcake and sprinkle with decorating sugar.
Yield: about 2 dozen cupcakes

If you're planning a party, treat your guests to dessert first with rich Double Chocolate Cupcakes in simple-to-make holders. Cheese Cookie Snacks only look like cookies—they're actually savory crackers with the mellow flavor of Cheddar.

Cupcake Place Card

• double-sided 12" x 12" cardstock • scallop-edged scissors • double-sided tape • alphabet stamps • ink pad • snowflake pick • Double Chocolate Cupcake

Enlarge patterns on page 151 to 200%. Use the patterns and cut a cardstock cupcake holder and a backdrop, scalloping the curved edge. Discard the cupcake opening piece. Fold on the dashed lines and tape the flaps to complete the holder. Tape the backdrop to the holder. Personalize a cardstock tag and tape to the holder front. Insert the snowflake pick in the cupcake and place the cupcake in the place card. ✷

Cheese Cookie Snacks

  1 cup (4 ounces) shredded Cheddar
       cheese
  $1/2$ cup butter or margarine, softened
  1 cup all-purpose flour
  $1/4$ teaspoon salt
  1 cup crisp rice cereal

Stir together cheese and butter until blended. Stir in flour and salt; blend well. Stir in cereal (dough will be stiff).

Shape dough into 1" balls; place on an ungreased baking sheet 2" apart. Flatten cookies to $1/4$" thickness with a fork, making a crisscross.

Bake in a preheated 350° oven for 12 to 15 minutes. Remove to wire rack to cool. Store in an airtight container.
Yield: about 2 dozen cookies

Snack Sleeve

• Cheese Cookie Snacks • cellophane • double-sided tape • ribbon • cardstock • seasonal sticker • adhesive foam dots • rub-on letters • linen thread • hole punch

1. Stack the desired number of cookie snacks. Overlapping and taping the edges at the back, wrap the cookies in cellophane; secure the ends with ribbon.
2. For the sleeve, cut cardstock to fit around the cookie stack plus 1". Wrap the sleeve around the snack stack and tape at the back.
3. For the greeting, add the sticker to a cardstock piece and use foam dots to adhere the greeting to the sleeve.
4. Cut a cardstock tag. Add "Cheese Cookie Snacks" to the tag with the rub-on letters. Knot linen thread through a hole in the tag; tie to the snack stack. ✳

Chip and Dip Bowl

To dress up this gift, add a ribbon, cardstock, and paper topper to the bag of chips and a tag to the jar of hummus. Fill the large bowl with excelsior; then, nestle a sparkly ornament in the bowl along with the snacks and ribbon-tied dipping bowl. ❊

Roasted Red Pepper Hummus and Garlic-Flavored Pita Chips

Hummus

  2 cans (15 ounces each) chickpeas
  1 jar (7 ounces) whole roasted red peppers in olive oil
  6 tablespoons lemon juice
$1/4$ cup tahini (sesame seed paste)
  2 garlic cloves, minced
$3/4$ teaspoon salt
$3/4$ teaspoon ground cumin
$1/2$ teaspoon ground cayenne pepper

Pita Chips

  5 pita breads, halved and split
$2/3$ cup olive oil
$1 1/2$ teaspoons garlic powder
$3/4$ teaspoon ground cumin
  2 tablespoons dried parsley flakes

    For hummus, purée all ingredients in a food processor until mixture is smooth, scraping the sides of the container several times. Store in an airtight container in the refrigerator for at least 1 hour to allow flavors to blend. (Hummus will keep in the refrigerator for 3 days.) Serve at room temperature.

    For pita chips, cut each pita half into 4 wedges. Place wedges on ungreased baking sheets. Combine oil, garlic powder, cumin, and parsley in a small bowl. Brush each wedge with oil mixture. Bake in a preheated 400° oven for 8 to 10 minutes or until lightly browned and crispy.

Yield: about 4 cups hummus and 80 pita chips

Spiced Pecans

- 3 tablespoons butter or margarine
- 1 tablespoon Worcestershire sauce
- 1/2 teaspoon garlic salt
- 1 pound pecan halves
- 1 teaspoon popcorn salt

   In a 5-quart sauce pan, melt butter and stir in Worcestershire sauce and garlic salt until well blended. Add pecan halves and stir to evenly coat. Spread pecans in a single layer on a cookie sheet. Sprinkle with popcorn salt. Bake in a preheated 250° oven for 30 minutes.

Yield: about 3 cups pecans
Contributed by Greg Sullivan

Gift Sack

- felt • pinking shears • ribbon
- fabric glue • fabric scraps
- 5/8" dia. covered button kit
- alphabet stamps • ink pad
- bagged Spiced Pecans

1. Matching the right sides and short ends, fold an 8" x 3½" felt piece in half. Using a ¼" seam allowance, sew the sides. Flatten and center each side seam against the bottom of the sack; sew across each corner 3/8" from the point (*Fig. 1*). Turn the sack right side out and pink the top edge. Glue ribbon around the sack top.
2. Enlarge the pattern on page 155 to 150%. Cut 2 fabric flowers. Cover the button with fabric. Sew the button and the

Some like it hot, so present them with a spicy gift bowl of Roasted Red Pepper Hummus and Garlic-Flavored Pita Chips. A tasty treat without the heat, Spiced Pecans are fun to present in a flower-embellished felt bag.

flowers to the sack. Stamp a pinked fabric scrap label and glue to the sack. Fill with a bag of Spiced Pecans.

Fig. 1

3/8"

food gifts ✳ 77

For the baker in your life, put together a clever cookie kit with supplies to make a fresh batch of Sugar Cookies.

Sugar Cookies
Bagged Ingredients
- 3/4 cup confectioners sugar
- 1 1/2 cups all-purpose flour
- 1/2 teaspoon baking soda
- 1/2 teaspoon cream of tartar
- 1 cup confectioners sugar
- Candy sprinkles

For the cookie mix, sift the first four ingredients together. Pour in a plastic resealable bag.

Pour 1 cup confectioners sugar in another resealable bag for frosting. Pour the sprinkles in a small resealable bag for the topping. Include the Sugar Cookie recipe, below, in the Holiday Cookie Kit.

Sugar Cookies
- Bagged Cookie Mix, Frosting and Topping
- 1/2 cup butter, softened
- 1 egg
- 1 teaspoon vanilla extract
- 1/2 teaspoon almond extract

Blend butter into cookie mix with a pastry blender. Stir the egg and extracts into the cookie mixture and blend the ingredients by hand. Cover the dough and chill. Roll the dough onto a floured surface to 1/4" thickness and cut out shapes. Bake in a preheated 375° oven on a lightly greased cookie sheet for 7 to 8 minutes or until the edges begin to brown. Cool on a wire rack.

Empty the frosting bag into a bowl and add 1 tablespoon water. Stir and add water as needed for spreading consistency. Tint frosting with food coloring, if desired. Frost the cookies and decorate with sprinkles.

Yield: about 2 1/2 to 3 dozen cookies

Holiday Cookie Kit

- 8" dia. cookie tin (ours has a lid with a clear plastic insert)
- Creative Paperclay® • large cookie cutter • alphabet stamps
- marker cap • acrylic paint and sponge brush • mica flakes
- cardstock • scallop-edged scissors • hole punch • ink pad
- tags • ribbons • red and green food coloring • cookie cutters to fit in tin

1. To make the label, cut ¼" thick rolled-out Paperclay with the large cookie cutter. Press the alphabet stamps into the clay to add the message. Make impressions in the clay for decoration (we used the end of a paintbrush, a pen cap, and a fancy button). Use the marker cap to cut 2 holes in the clay for the ribbon to run through. Allow the clay to dry for a day. Lightly paint the clay and while it is wet, sprinkle with mica flakes.

2. Cut a folded cardstock topper with scalloped edges for each ingredient bag. Punch holes through each topper and bag (above the closure), add a stamped tag, and tie with ribbon.

3. Cut 2 scalloped cardstock circles slightly smaller than the bottom of the tin. Place one in the tin with the recipe, bags, and food coloring. Add the remaining circle, the cookie cutters, and the lid. Tie the label around the tin with ribbon. ✼

Breakfast is served, and today it's quick, grab-and-go Pancake Mini Muffins and a bottle of maple syrup for the recipient who's always on the run. A box of Chocolate Bon-bons is a gift that truly pampers.

Pancake Mini Muffins

- 2 cups pancake mix
- 1 cup milk
- 1/4 cup maple syrup
- 1 egg, beaten
- 1 teaspoon maple flavoring
- 2 tablespoons sugar
- 1 teaspoon ground cinnamon

Whisk together first 5 ingredients until no lumps remain. Line mini muffin pans with paper baking cups; fill cups 1/2 full. Combine sugar and cinnamon, mixing well. Sprinkle sugar mixture over muffin batter. Bake in a preheated 350° oven for 5 to 7 minutes or until a toothpick inserted in center comes out clean. Remove from pans and cool on wire racks. **Yield:** about 3 1/2 dozen mini muffins

Mini Muffin Gift Set

- kitchen towel • covered button kit • fabric scraps
- assorted sizes of rickrack
- glass bottle of maple syrup
- packaged Pancake Mini Muffins

Cover buttons with fabric. Sew rickrack and buttons to one end of the towel. Secure a rickrack length around the bottle with a button. Give with muffins. ❋

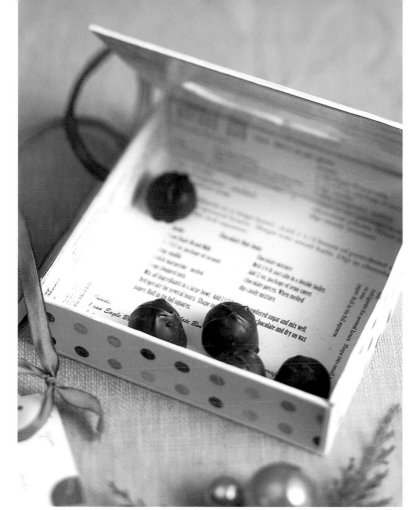

Candy Box
• 6¼" square box with lid cutout (we found ours at a scrapbook store) • recipe or holiday scrapbook paper to line box • craft glue • double-sided tape • clear acetate sheet • scrapbook paper • white or colored tape • Chocolate Bon-bons • ribbon • hole punch • linen twine

Line the inside of the box with scrapbook paper or use different fonts to make a collage of the bon-bon recipe; then, tape acetate inside the lid. Cover the outside of the box with scrapbook papers and the corners with white or colored tape. Fill the box with candy. Tie a ribbon around the box. Make a scrapbook paper tag and use twine to tie it to the ribbon. ❊

Chocolate Bon-bons
1 can (14 ounces) sweetened condensed milk
1 package (7½ ounces) sweetened shredded coconut
1 teaspoon vanilla extract
½ cup margarine, melted
1 cup chopped nuts
1½ packages (16 ounces each) confectioners sugar
1 cup semi-sweet chocolate chips
6 ounces chocolate candy coating

Mix first 5 ingredients in a large bowl. Add confectioners sugar and mix well. Refrigerate for several hours.

Melt chocolate chips and candy coating in the top of a double boiler. Shape coconut mixture into small balls and dip into melted chocolate mixture. Place on wax paper to harden. Wrap in foil squares, if desired.
Yield: about 5½ dozen bon-bons

Sweet Potato Casserole

  2 cans (29 ounces each) sweet potatoes in syrup,
      drained and mashed (about 4 cups mashed)
  6 tablespoons melted butter, divided
$1/2$ cup granulated sugar
  1 can (8 ounces) crushed pineapple, drained
  1 cup firmly packed light brown sugar, divided
  2 eggs, lightly beaten
  1 teaspoon vanilla extract
$1/2$ teaspoon ground cinnamon
$1/4$ teaspoon ground nutmeg
$1/3$ cup evaporated milk
$3/4$ cup chopped pecans
$1/4$ cup all-purpose flour

Combine sweet potatoes, 4 tablespoons butter, granulated sugar, pineapple, $1/4$ cup brown sugar, eggs, vanilla, and spices in a large bowl; beat at medium speed with an electric mixer until smooth. Add evaporated milk; stir well. Pour into a lightly greased 9" x 13" baking dish.

Combine remaining 2 tablespoons butter, remaining $3/4$ cup brown sugar, pecans, and flour in a small bowl. Sprinkle over sweet potatoes.

Bake in a preheated 350° oven for 35 to 40 minutes or until heated through and edges are bubbly.
Yield: 8 servings

Help a busy cook this Christmas by preparing a Sweet Potato Casserole for his or her dining table. The traditional dish looks merry and stays warm in an easy-sew cozy.

Casserole Cozy
fits a 9" x 13" baking dish
• two $15^{1}/_{2}$" x $19^{1}/_{2}$" coordinating fabric pieces • two $15^{1}/_{2}$" x $19^{1}/_{2}$" low-loft polyester bonded batting pieces • four $7/8$" dia. buttons

1. Place the fabric pieces right sides together on top of the stacked batting pieces. Leaving an opening for turning, use a $1/2$" seam allowance and stitch all layers together. Clip the corners diagonally, turn right side out, and press; sew the opening closed.
2. Stitch 3" from each edge of the cozy.
3. Fold fabric up along the stitched lines, matching the lines to form each corner. Tack the sides together at each corner. Fold each fabric point toward the center and tack. Sew a button to each corner. Place the baked casserole in the cozy. ✳

Chocolate-Caramel Pretzel Sticks

- 20 caramels, unwrapped
- 1 tablespoon milk
- 10 pretzel sticks
  Chocolate and white candy coating
  Chopped nuts, crushed peppermint candy, sprinkles

Place caramels and milk in an 8-ounce glass measuring cup and melt in the microwave on HIGH for 30 to 45 seconds or until the mixture starts to bubble. Stir until smooth and let cool slightly. Dip pretzels in the caramel about halfway up the stick. Let the excess drip back into the measuring cup; then place pretzels in short juice glasses, dipped end up (be careful not to let the them touch each other). Let the caramel set up to a firm consistency (about 10 minutes).

Place 2 ounces of chocolate candy coating in a microwave-safe glass bowl and microwave on HIGH for 30 seconds; stir. Heat for 30 more seconds and stir. Spoon chocolate onto the coated pretzels, covering the caramel; let the excess drip into the bowl and replace the pretzels in the juice glasses.

When slightly cool, roll pretzels in nuts, crushed peppermints, or sprinkles. Or, melt white candy coating in a microwave-safe glass bowl on HIGH for 30 seconds; stir. Heat for 30 more seconds and stir. Spoon white candy coating into a plastic bag. Cut off a corner and drizzle coating over the chocolate.

Yield: 10 chocolate-caramel pretzel sticks

Pretzel Glasses

- drinking glasses • assorted cardstock • double-sided tape • pinking shears • rub-on letters • large needle • brads • ribbon • printed food-safe tissue paper • Chocolate-Caramel Pretzel Sticks

1. For each gift, cut a piece of cardstock to fit around the glass plus 1". Overlapping and taping the edges at the back, wrap the cardstock piece around the glass.
2. Enlarge the patterns on page 155 to 169%. Use the patterns and cut the ovals, pinking the edges of the smaller one. Layer and tape the ovals; then, add a rub-on monogram. Center the tag on the ribbon and use the needle to pierce both; then, insert the brads into the holes. Tie the tag around the glass and add tissue before adding pretzel sticks. ✳

Tex-Mex Seasoning

Multiply the recipe as desired.

    3 tablespoons chili powder
    2 tablespoons ground cumin
    1 tablespoon ground black
       pepper
    1 tablespoon salt
    1 tablespoon garlic powder
1½ teaspoons ground red
       pepper

Stir together all ingredients and store in an airtight container up to 6 months. Sprinkle on chicken, beef, potatoes, corn, and popped popcorn.

Yield: about ½ cup seasoning

Seasoning Wrap

• cardstock • scallop-edged scissors • Tex-Mex Seasoning in a resealable bag • ¼" dia. hole punch • ribbon • alphabet stamps • ink pad • craft glue • letter stickers • brad • fine glitter • adhesive foam dots

1. For the wrap, cut a 7" x 11" cardstock piece. Fold 4½" from each short end; unfold.
2. For the topper, match long edges and fold a 4" x 7" cardstock piece in half. Scallop the long edges.
3. Place the plastic bag in the wrap, aligning the top edges. Place the topper over the wrap and punch 2 holes through all layers (above the closure). Tie a bow, threading the ribbon through both holes. Stamp "seasoning" on a cardstock strip. Glue the strip near the wrap bottom. Adhere stickers to the wrap.
4. Cut a cardstock tag and "reinforcing" circle. Stamp a message on the tag. Layer the circle and the tag on the wrap and attach with a brad, inserting the brad through the punched holes.
5. Enlarge the patterns, page 154, to 145%; using the patterns, cut cardstock jalapeño pieces. Apply glitter to the pepper; glue the cap to the top. Attach the jalapeño with foam dots. ✳

You'll want to make extra Chocolate-Caramel Pretzel Sticks—they're simply irresistible! Christmas is a wonderful time to add the zip of Tex-Mex Seasoning to ordinary meals.

Garlic Vinegar

- 4 cups (32 ounces) red wine vinegar
- 4 garlic cloves, peeled and trimmed to fit in bottle

Wooden skewer to fit in bottle

In a saucepan, bring vinegar to a boil; remove from heat. Thread garlic cloves on skewer; carefully insert in a sterilized bottle. Pour vinegar in bottle; cap. Refrigerate at least 2 days to allow flavors to blend. Store in refrigerator and use within 3 weeks.

Yield: 32 ounces

Herbed Lemon Vinegar

- 4 cups (32 ounces) white wine vinegar
- 4 lemons
- 4 small sprigs fresh dill, basil, or tarragon

In a saucepan, bring vinegar to a boil; remove from heat. Using paring knife, peel each lemon in a continuous spiral. Place lemon peel and herb sprigs in a sterilized bottle. Pour vinegar in bottle; cap. Refrigerate at least 2 days to allow flavors to blend. Store in refrigerator and use within 3 weeks.

Yield: 32 ounces

Blueberry Vinegar

- 2 cups frozen blueberries, thawed
- 4 cups (32 ounces) rice wine vinegar

In a saucepan, combine 1 cup berries with vinegar. Heat for 10 minutes, but do not boil. Place remaining berries in a sterilized bottle. Straining vinegar through a fine strainer, pour vinegar in bottle; cap. Store in refrigerator and use within 3 weeks.

Yield: 32 ounces

These zesty vinegars wake up salads and vegetables with new flavors.

Bottle Tags

Cover a chipboard snowflake with patterned scrapbook paper and glitter the edges for a sparkly touch. Attach the snowflake to the bottle with a ribbon loop; a pretty silver button glued to the center completes the look. ❄

creating good *food* for the HOLIDAYS

At this time of year, you look forward to gathering with loved ones and *celebrating* with friends. That's why we've put together this *special selection* of recipes. The best appetizers, soups, meals, and desserts are now at your fingertips. *Merry Christmas!*

appetizers & beverages

Exceptional foods like Cheesy Crab Puffs and Herbed Pimiento Dip are an important part of everyone's Christmas celebrations. In these pages, you'll find an amazing array of spreads, finger foods, and snacks, as well as warm and chilled beverages. For all your Yuletide get-togethers, you now have the perfect recipes!

Cheesy Crab Puffs

- 1 can (6 ounces) crabmeat, drained
- 4 ounces cream cheese, softened
- 1 cup (4 ounces) shredded Swiss cheese
- 1/4 cup finely chopped red pepper (we used equal amounts of sweet and jalapeño peppers)
- 2 tablespoons finely chopped green onions
- 2 tablespoons purchased plain bread crumbs
- 1 teaspoon freshly squeezed lemon juice
- 1 teaspoon prepared horseradish
- 1 teaspoon Worcestershire sauce
- 1/2 teaspoon garlic salt
- 1/8 teaspoon ground red pepper
- 1 package (17 1/4 ounces) frozen puff pastry, thawed according to package directions

In a medium bowl, combine crabmeat, cream cheese, Swiss cheese, chopped red pepper, green onions, bread crumbs, lemon juice, horseradish, Worcestershire sauce, garlic salt, and ground red pepper; beat until well blended. On a lightly floured surface, use a floured rolling pin to roll each pastry sheet into a 10" square. Cut pastry into 2" squares. Press a pastry square into each ungreased cup of a non-stick miniature muffin pan. Spoon 1 teaspoon crab mixture into center of each square. Bake in a preheated 400° oven for 19 to 21 minutes or until golden brown. Serve warm.

Yield: about 4 dozen puffs ❋

Herbed Pimiento Dip

- 1 container (8 ounces) fat-free sour cream
- 4 ounces fat-free cream cheese, softened
- 1/2 cup fat-free mayonnaise
- 1 clove garlic, minced
- 1 jar (7 ounces) sliced pimientos, drained
- 1 tablespoon chopped fresh basil leaves
- 1 tablespoon chopped fresh oregano leaves
- 1 teaspoon lemon pepper
- 1/2 teaspoon salt
- Fresh vegetables to serve

Process sour cream, cream cheese, mayonnaise, and garlic in a food processor until smooth. Add pimientos, basil, oregano, lemon pepper, and salt. Pulse process until blended. Transfer to a serving bowl. Cover and refrigerate 2 hours to let flavors blend. Serve with vegetables.

Yield: about 2 1/2 cups dip ❋

Cheesy Crab Puffs
Herbed Pimiento Dip

Cheese Spreads

Basic Spread

- 2 packages (8 ounces each) cream cheese, softened
- 1/2 cup sour cream
- 3 tablespoons mayonnaise

Beat cream cheese, sour cream, and mayonnaise in a medium bowl until smooth. Use Basic Spread to make each of the following recipes.
Yield: about 2 2/3 cups spread

Cheese Spreads

GARLIC

1 cup Basic Spread
1 1/2 teaspoons garlic salt
1 teaspoon fines herbes
1/8 teaspoon hot pepper sauce
Garnish: fines herbes
Assorted crackers to serve

Combine basic spread, garlic salt, 1 teaspoon fines herbes, and pepper sauce in a small bowl; stir until well blended. Transfer to a serving container; garnish, if desired. Serve with assorted crackers.

CHEESE

1 cup Basic Spread
1/3 cup grated Parmesan cheese
1 teaspoon Worcestershire sauce
3/4 teaspoon onion salt
Garnish: grated Parmesan cheese
Assorted crackers to serve

Combine basic spread, 1/3 cup Parmesan cheese, Worcestershire sauce, and onion salt; stir until well blended. Transfer to a serving container; garnish, if desired. Serve with assorted crackers.

ALMOND

2/3 cup Basic Spread
1/4 cup butter, softened
1/4 cup sugar
1/8 cup golden raisins
1/8 cup slivered almonds, lightly toasted
Garnish: raisins and almonds
Assorted crackers to serve

Combine basic spread, butter, sugar, 1/8 cup raisins, and 1/8 cup almonds; stir until well blended. Transfer to a serving container; garnish, if desired. Serve with assorted crackers. ❋

Mushroom Pillows

1 pound fresh mushrooms
3 tablespoons butter
1 tablespoon vegetable oil
1/4 cup finely chopped green onions
2 cloves garlic, minced
2 tablespoons dry white wine
1 teaspoon chopped fresh thyme leaves
1/2 teaspoon salt
1/2 teaspoon ground black pepper
4 ounces cream cheese, softened
1 package (12 ounces) wonton wrappers
Vegetable oil

Process mushrooms in a food processor until finely chopped. Melt butter with 1 tablespoon oil in a large skillet over medium heat. Add mushrooms, green onions, and garlic; sauté about 20 minutes or until liquid from mushrooms evaporates. Stirring constantly, add wine and cook until liquid evaporates. Stir in thyme, salt, and pepper. Remove from heat and add cream cheese; stir until melted. Place 1 teaspoon mixture on lower half of each wonton wrapper. Brush edges with water; fold sides over filling. Fold lower edge of wrapper over filling and roll. Press edges to seal. Place, seam side down, on baking sheet. Cover and refrigerate until ready to serve.

To serve, deep fry appetizers in hot oil until browned, about 1 to 2 minutes. Drain on paper towels. Serve warm.
Yield: about 4 dozen appetizers ❋

Make just one mellow Cheese Spread, or all three of its easy variations. Serve them with crackers or bagel crisps. The Almond Cheese Spread is lightly sweet and especially good with graham crackers.

Sweet-and-sour Marmalade Meatballs can be prepared in advance and reheated before serving. Ground red pepper gives Cheesy Miniature Quiches extra zip.

Marmalade Meatballs

Marmalade Meatballs

- 1 egg
- 1/2 cup water
- 1 pound finely ground chuck
- 1 cup water chestnuts, finely chopped
- 1/2 cup bread crumbs
- 2 teaspoons horseradish
- 1/4 teaspoon salt
- 2/3 cup orange marmalade
- 1/3 cup water
- 2 tablespoons soy sauce
- 2 tablespoons lemon juice
- 1 clove garlic, finely minced

In a medium bowl, beat egg and 1/2 cup water. Blend in ground chuck, water chestnuts, bread crumbs, horseradish, and salt. (**Note:** For tender meatballs, do not overmix.) Shape mixture into 3/4" balls. Place meatballs on a foil-lined baking sheet. Bake in a preheated 350° oven for 30 minutes or until lightly browned.

While meatballs are cooking, make sauce by combining remaining ingredients in a saucepan. Heat slowly, stirring often.

Place cooked meatballs in a serving dish and cover with sauce.

Yield: about 24 servings ❋

Cheesy Miniature Quiches

- 2 cups all-purpose flour
- $\frac{1}{2}$ cup butter or margarine, melted
- $1\frac{1}{2}$ teaspoons salt
- $\frac{3}{4}$ teaspoon ground red pepper
- 4 cups (16 ounces) shredded sharp Cheddar cheese
- 4 eggs
- $\frac{3}{4}$ cup milk
- 8 ounces bacon, cooked and crumbled
- $\frac{1}{2}$ cup frozen chopped spinach, thawed and squeezed dry
- Optional garnishes: cucumber slices, carrot curls, green onion tops and curls, red onion, tomato peel, sweet red pepper, dill weed, and celery leaves and slices

Cheesy Miniature Quiches

Process flour, melted butter, salt, and red pepper in a food processor until combined. Add cheese; process until well blended. Shape dough into $1\frac{1}{2}$" balls. Press dough into bottom and up sides of greased $2\frac{1}{2}$" tart pans.

In a medium bowl, whisk eggs and milk. Stir in bacon and spinach. Spoon 1 tablespoon filling into each pastry shell. Bake in a preheated 350° oven for 20 to 25 minutes or until center is set. Cool in pans 5 minutes. Remove from pans; garnish, if desired. Serve warm.
Yield: about 3 dozen quiches ❄

Roasted Red Pepper Dip

- 2 large sweet red peppers
- $\frac{1}{2}$ cup fat-free mayonnaise
- $\frac{1}{2}$ cup fat-free sour cream
- 1 tablespoon minced onion
- 2 teaspoons chopped fresh parsley
- 1 small clove garlic, minced
- $\frac{1}{2}$ teaspoon white wine vinegar
- $\frac{1}{4}$ teaspoon ground white pepper
- $\frac{1}{4}$ teaspoon celery salt
- $\frac{1}{4}$ teaspoon salt
- Low-fat crackers to serve

To roast red peppers, cut in half lengthwise and remove seeds and membranes. Place skin side up on an ungreased baking sheet; use hand to flatten peppers. Broil about 3" from heat about 10 minutes or until peppers are blackened and charred. Immediately seal peppers in a resealable plastic bag and allow to steam 10 to 15 minutes. Remove charred skin and finely chop peppers.

In a medium bowl, combine chopped roasted red peppers, mayonnaise, sour cream, onion, parsley, garlic, vinegar, white pepper, celery salt, and salt. Stir until well blended. Cover and chill 1 hour to allow flavors to blend. Serve at room temperature with crackers.
Yield: about 2 cups dip ❄

Christmas Pasta Snacks

Savory Tomato and Olive Pastries

   6 ounces cream cheese, softened
 1/3 cup finely chopped green onions
 1/3 cup finely chopped fresh mushrooms
 1/2 teaspoon ground black pepper
   1 sheet frozen puff pastry, thawed
   6 ounces thinly sliced Provolone cheese
 3/4 cup dried tomatoes marinated in olive oil, drained and cut into strips
   1 can (2 1/4 ounces) sliced black olives, drained

In a medium bowl, beat cream cheese until fluffy. Stir in green onions, mushrooms, and pepper. On a lightly floured surface, use a lightly floured rolling pin to roll out pastry into a 10 1/2" square. Cut pastry in half. Transfer pastry pieces to an ungreased baking sheet. Dampen edges of pastries with water. Fold edges of pastries 1/2" toward center and press to seal. Spread cream cheese mixture over pastries. Place cheese slices over cream cheese mixture. Add tomatoes and olives. Bake in a preheated 400° oven for 15 to 17 minutes or until cheese melts and pastries are golden brown. Let stand 5 minutes. Cut each pastry in half lengthwise, then cut into 1" slices. Serve warm.
Yield: about 3 dozen appetizers ❄

Christmas Pasta Snacks and Seafood-Stuffed Jalapeños are a feast of amazing flavors. You'll find the recipe for zesty Citrus Cider Punch on page 103.

Christmas Pasta Snacks
   2 tablespoons grated Parmesan cheese
   1 teaspoon ground cumin
 3/4 teaspoon ground oregano
 3/4 teaspoon salt
 1/2 teaspoon garlic powder
     Vegetable oil
   8 ounces tree-shaped pasta, cooked, drained, and patted dry

Lightly grease a sheet of aluminum foil; set aside.
In a small bowl, combine cheese, cumin, oregano, salt, and garlic powder; set aside. In a heavy medium saucepan, heat oil to 375°. Stirring occasionally, deep fry 1 cup pasta 4 to 5 minutes or until pasta is golden brown and oil stops bubbling. Drain on paper towels. Transfer warm pasta to aluminum foil. Sprinkle about 2 teaspoons cheese mixture over warm pasta. Repeat with remaining pasta and cheese mixture. Cool completely and store in an airtight container.
Yield: about 4 1/2 cups snack mix ❄

Seafood-Stuffed Jalapeños

Horseradish Sauce

1½ cups sour cream
¾ cup mayonnaise
4 to 5 tablespoons prepared horseradish

Peppers

30 medium jalapeño peppers
1 package (8 ounces) cream cheese, softened
1 can (6 ounces) small shrimp, drained
1 can (6 ounces) crabmeat, drained
2 tablespoons finely chopped onion
1 tablespoon Worcestershire sauce
1 tablespoon freshly squeezed lemon juice
¼ teaspoon garlic powder
1 cup buttermilk
1 egg, beaten
½ cup corn flake crumbs
¾ cup self-rising cornmeal mix
Vegetable oil

For horseradish sauce, combine sour cream, mayonnaise, and horseradish in a small bowl. Cover and chill 4 hours to let flavors blend.

For peppers, cut peppers in half lengthwise and seed (protect hands with gloves). To blanch peppers, cover with water in a large saucepan. Cover and bring to a boil over medium-high heat; boil 5 minutes. Being careful to avoid steam, drain peppers and rinse with cold water. Drain on paper towels.

In a medium bowl, combine cream cheese, shrimp, crabmeat, onion, Worcestershire sauce, lemon juice, and garlic powder; beat until well blended. Transfer cream cheese mixture to a quart-size resealable plastic bag. Cut off 1 corner of bag and pipe mixture into each pepper half. Place on a baking sheet lined with waxed paper; freeze about 1 hour or until filling is frozen.

Combine buttermilk and egg in a small bowl. In a medium bowl, combine corn flake crumbs and cornmeal mix. Dip each pepper into buttermilk mixture and roll in crumb mixture. Return to baking sheet. Cover and freeze 1 hour.

To serve, heat oil to 350° in a heavy medium saucepan. Removing about 6 peppers at a time from freezer, deep fry peppers about 2 minutes or until golden brown. Drain on paper towels. Serve warm with sauce.

Yield: about 2½ cups sauce and 5 dozen appetizers ❋

Citrus Cider Punch (recipe on page 103)
Seafood-Stuffed Jalapeños

Cherry Salsa

Cherry Salsa

2 cans (15 ounces each) dark, sweet, pitted cherries in heavy syrup, drained and coarsely chopped
3 tablespoons chopped red onion
3 tablespoons chopped fresh basil leaves
3 tablespoons finely chopped green pepper
3 tablespoons honey
2 tablespoons finely chopped fresh jalapeño pepper
1 tablespoon freshly squeezed lemon juice
1 teaspoon grated lemon zest
¹/₂ teaspoon salt
Tortilla chips to serve

In a medium bowl, combine cherries, onion, basil, green pepper, honey, jalapeño pepper, lemon juice, lemon zest, and salt. Cover and chill 2 hours to let flavors blend. Serve salsa with tortilla chips.
Yield: about 2 cups salsa ✻

Want to serve unique dips that will disappear in record time? Sweet/hot Cherry Salsa and Smoked Oyster Spread are hard to resist. For hearty snacking, bake a quick batch of Spicy Pastrami Rolls. Fragrant with cloves, allspice, and cinnamon, Hot Cranberry Punch (recipe, page 103) is a true taste of the season!

Spicy Pastrami Rolls

2 cans (8 ounces each) refrigerated crescent rolls
1/2 pound deli pastrami, thinly sliced
1/2 cup soft cream cheese with chives and onions
1/3 cup Dijon-style mustard

Separate crescent rolls into triangles. Cut triangles in half to make 2 smaller triangles. Cut pastrami into 1" x 2" strips. Spread 1 teaspoon cream cheese and 1/2 teaspoon mustard on each triangle, leaving about 1/4" of the pointed end uncovered. Stack 3 pieces of pastrami at wide end of the triangle. Beginning at the wide end, roll up triangle and place on an ungreased baking sheet with point side down. Bake in a preheated 375° oven for 12 to 15 minutes or until golden brown. Serve warm.
Yield: 32 appetizers ❄

Smoked Oyster Spread

2 packages (8 ounces each) cream cheese, softened
1/4 cup chopped green onions
2 tablespoons mayonnaise
1 tablespoon lemon juice
2 teaspoons prepared horseradish
2 teaspoons Worcestershire sauce
1/2 teaspoon salt
1/4 teaspoon onion powder
1/4 teaspoon hot pepper sauce
2 cans (3.6 ounces each) smoked oysters, drained and chopped
Crackers to serve

In a large mixing bowl, beat cream cheese until smooth. Add next 8 ingredients, mixing well. Stir in oysters. Cover and chill 8 hours or overnight. Serve with crackers.
Yield: about 3 cups spread ❄

Spicy Pastrami Rolls
Smoked Oyster Spread

Hot Cranberry Punch
(recipe on page 103)

Everyone will love these unforgettable flavors! Nutty Blue Cheese Spread and Green Olive and Jalapeño Roll-ups are truly simple to prepare. Hot Spiced Fruit Tea will charm your guests with the unexpected combination of lemon and ginger.

Hot Spiced Fruit Tea
Nutty Blue Cheese Spread
Green Olive and Jalapeño Roll-ups

Nutty Blue Cheese Spread

1 package (8 ounces) cream cheese, softened
1 package (4 ounces) blue cheese, crumbled
2 tablespoons sour cream
1/4 teaspoon ground red pepper
1/4 cup finely chopped celery
1/4 cup finely chopped green onions
1 1/2 cups chopped walnuts, toasted, finely chopped, and divided
   Crackers to serve

Process cream cheese, blue cheese, sour cream, and red pepper in a food processor until smooth. Add celery, green onions, and 1 cup walnuts; process just until blended. Transfer to a 2 1/2-cup serving container. Cover with plastic wrap and chill 2 hours to let flavors blend.

To serve, bring cheese spread to room temperature. Sprinkle with remaining 1/2 cup walnuts. Serve with crackers.
Yield: about 2 1/4 cups spread ❄

Green Olive and Jalapeño Roll-ups

1 package (8 ounces) cream cheese, softened
1/2 cup mayonnaise
1 cup sliced pimiento-stuffed olives, chopped
1/2 cup chopped pecans, toasted and finely chopped
1 1/2 tablespoons chopped pickled jalapeño peppers
4 (12" dia.) flavored tortilla wraps (we used spinach-herb and tomato-basil flavors)

In a medium bowl, combine cream cheese and mayonnaise; beat until smooth. Add olives, pecans, and jalapeño peppers; stir until well blended. Spread about 1/2 cup mixture onto each tortilla. Tightly roll up tortillas and wrap in plastic wrap. Chill 2 hours. Cut into 1/2" slices.
Yield: about 7 1/2 dozen roll-ups ❄

Hot Spiced Fruit Tea

1 bottle (64 ounces) apple juice
4 cups water
1 can (6 ounces) frozen lemonade concentrate, thawed
10 orange-spiced tea bags
1 piece (2" long) fresh ginger, peeled and thinly sliced
1/2 cup firmly packed brown sugar
   Lemon slices to serve

Combine apple juice, water, and lemonade concentrate in a Dutch oven. Add tea bags and ginger slices. Bring to a simmer over medium-high heat. Reduce heat to low; cover and simmer 15 minutes. Remove tea bags and ginger. Stir in brown sugar. Simmer 10 minutes. Serve warm with lemon slices.
Yield: about 12 cups tea ❄

Raspberry Liqueur

2 packages (10 ounces each) frozen raspberries in syrup, thawed
1 1/2 cups sugar
1/2 lemon, sliced
1 1/2 cups vodka

Drain juice from raspberries into large saucepan; reserve raspberries.

Combine sugar and lemon slices with raspberry juice.

Stirring often, bring mixture to a boil over low heat; remove from heat.

Skim any foam from top of mixture and remove lemon slices. Stir in raspberries and vodka to juice mixture. Fill bottle; cap. Store in refrigerator for one month before serving, shaking bottle every week to mix contents. Before serving, pour contents through a fine strainer. Store in refrigerator after opening.
Yield: about 24 ounces liqueur❄

appetizers & beverages ❄

Southern Eggnog
Chocolate Eggnog

Southern Eggnog

Our eggnog begins with a cooked custard made in advance. We've also included a version for those who prefer eggnog without alcohol.

- 1 cup sugar, divided
- 12 large eggs, separated
- 1/2 teaspoon salt
- 1 quart milk
- 1/4 cup water
- 3/4 teaspoon cream of tartar
- 2 cups whipping cream
- 1/2 cup brandy
- 1/2 cup dark rum
  Garnish: freshly grated nutmeg

In the top of a double boiler, combine 1/2 cup sugar, egg yolks, and salt. Gradually stir in milk. Cook over simmering water until mixture thickens and coats the back of a metal spoon. Remove from heat and cool. Pour mixture into an airtight container and chill.

In the top of a double boiler, combine egg whites, remaining 1/2 cup sugar, water, and cream of tartar. Whisking constantly, cook over simmering water until a thermometer reaches 160° (about 10 minutes). Transfer egg white mixture to a large bowl; beat until stiff peaks form. Cover and chill mixture.

In another large bowl, beat whipping cream until stiff peaks form. Pour egg yolk mixture into punch bowl. Stir in brandy and rum. Fold in egg white mixture and whipped cream. Garnish, if desired. (For eggnog without alcohol, substitute alcohol with 2 teaspoons rum extract and 1 cup whipping cream.)
Yield: about 3 1/2 quarts eggnog ❄

Chocolate Eggnog

- 1 quart purchased eggnog
- 1/2 cup chocolate syrup
- 1/4 teaspoon ground nutmeg
- 1 tablespoon vanilla extract
  Garnish: ground nutmeg

In a large saucepan, combine eggnog, chocolate syrup, and 1/4 teaspoon nutmeg. Stirring occasionally, cook over medium-low heat 20 to 25 minutes or until heated through (do not boil). Remove from heat; stir in vanilla. To serve, pour into cups; garnish, if desired. Serve warm.
Yield: six 6-ounce servings ❄

Cherry-Berry Cider

- 1 package (12 ounces) frozen whole blackberries
- 1 package (12 ounces) frozen whole dark sweet cherries
- 3 cinnamon sticks
- 2 teaspoons whole allspice
- 1 gallon apple cider
  Cinnamon sticks to serve

In a Dutch oven, combine blackberries, cherries, 3 cinnamon sticks, and allspice. Add apple cider. Bring to a simmer over medium-high heat. Use a potato masher to mash fruit. Reduce heat to medium; cover and simmer 30 minutes. Strain mixture and serve warm with cinnamon sticks.
Yield: about 16 1/2 cups cider ❄

It isn't Christmas without these creamy beverages! Southern Eggnog gets its delightful accent from a little brandy and rum, while Chocolate Eggnog is a special treat for guests of all ages.

Irish Smoothie
Chocolate Cups

Irish Smoothie

- 2 cups whipping cream
- 1 cup sweetened condensed milk
- ³/₄ cup Irish whiskey
- ¹/₂ cup brandy
- 2 tablespoons chocolate syrup
- 1 tablespoon instant coffee granules
- 1 teaspoon vanilla extract
- 1 teaspoon almond extract

Combine whipping cream, condensed milk, whiskey, brandy, chocolate syrup, coffee granules, and extracts in a blender until well mixed. Cover and store in refrigerator.
Yield: about 4¹/₄ cups liqueur ❋

CHOCOLATE CUPS

- 4 squares (1 ounce each) semisweet baking chocolate
- 1 tablespoon butter
- 8 foil muffin cup liners
  Ice cream, Irish Smoothie, and fresh sweet cherries to serve

In a heavy small saucepan, melt chocolate and butter over low heat, stirring constantly (do not overheat). Cool until slightly thickened. Place 1 tablespoon chocolate mixture in a foil cup; spread over bottom and sides. Place another foil cup on top of chocolate and press lightly. Repeat with remaining chocolate mixture. Refrigerate or freeze until firm.
To serve, carefully remove foil liners. Fill each chocolate cup with ice cream; drizzle with Irish Smoothie and top with a cherry.
Yield: 4 chocolate cups ❋

Wine Cooler

1 gallon red Zinfandel wine
1 quart orange juice
1 cup lemon juice
1/2 cup sugar
1 quart club soda, chilled
Garnish: orange slices

In a large container, combine wine, juices, and sugar. Stir until sugar is dissolved. Chill completely.

When ready to serve, add club soda. Serve over ice and garnish, if desired.
Yield: about 1 1/2 gallons wine cooler ❊

Cranberry-Champagne Cocktail

1/4 cup cranberry-flavored liqueur
2 tablespoons orange-flavored liqueur
1 tablespoon sweet vermouth
1 bottle (750 ml) champagne, chilled

In a 2-quart container, combine liqueurs and vermouth. Add champagne to mixture. Serve immediately.
Yield: about 3 1/2 cups cocktail ❊

Hot Cranberry Punch
Shown on page 97

6 cups cranberry juice
4 cups orange juice
1 cup water
1 can (6 ounces) frozen lemonade concentrate, thawed
1/2 cup firmly packed brown sugar
3 teaspoons whole cloves
3 teaspoons ground allspice
1 whole nutmeg, crushed
4 3" long cinnamon sticks, broken into pieces
Cinnamon sticks to serve

In a large saucepan or Dutch oven, combine first 5 ingredients. Place spices in a piece of cheesecloth and tie with string; add to punch. Bring mixture to a boil, stirring occasionally. Reduce to low heat, cover, and simmer 30 minutes. Serve hot with cinnamon sticks.
Yield: about 3 quarts punch ❊

Citrus Cider Punch
Shown on page 95

1 gallon apple cider, chilled
1 can (12 ounces) frozen limeade concentrate, thawed
1 can (12 ounces) frozen lemonade concentrate, thawed
1 bottle (2 liters) lemon-lime soda, chilled
Garnish: lemon and lime slices and maraschino cherries with stems

In a 2-gallon container, mix cider and concentrates. Stir in soda. Garnish, if desired. Serve immediately.
Yield: about 27 cups punch ❊

Irish Smoothie is a chocolaty indulgence that doubles as a rich ice cream topping.

❄ *soups & breads* ❄

Nothing chases the chill of winter like hot soup and home-baked bread! Whether you're cooking for family, houseguests, or holiday potlucks, these reliable recipes are the ones you'll turn to each year. For a fast and flavorful meal, try simple Butter-Me-Nots and Quick Bean Soup.

Butter-Me-Nots

  2 cups self-rising flour
  1 cup sour cream
  1 cup butter, melted

   Combine all ingredients. Spoon batter into lightly greased mini muffin pans, filling full. Bake in a preheated 400° oven for 15 minutes or until golden.
Yield: about 3 dozen ❄

Quick Bean Soup

  1 large onion, chopped
  1 small green bell pepper, chopped
  2 teaspoons vegetable oil
  1 can (16 ounces) kidney beans, rinsed and drained
  1 can (15 ounces) pinto beans, rinsed and drained
  1 can (15 ounces) black beans, rinsed and drained
  2 cans (14^1/$_2$ ounces each) stewed tomatoes, undrained
  1 can (14^1/$_2$ ounces) chicken broth
  1 cup picante sauce
  1 teaspoon ground cumin

   Sauté onion and bell pepper in hot oil in a large saucepan until tender. Add kidney beans and remaining ingredients; bring to a boil. Cover, reduce heat, and simmer 10 minutes.
Yield: about 10 cups soup ❄

Creamy Corn Muffins
Shown on page 106

  1 cup yellow cornmeal
  1 cup all-purpose flour
  2 tablespoons sugar
  1 tablespoon baking powder
  ^{3}/$_4$ teaspoon salt
  ^{1}/$_2$ teaspoon baking soda
  1 can (8^1/$_2$ ounces) cream-style corn
  1 cup sour cream
  ^{1}/$_4$ cup butter or margarine, melted
  1 egg

   In a medium bowl, combine cornmeal, flour, sugar, baking powder, salt, and baking soda. In a small bowl, beat corn, sour cream, melted butter, and egg until well blended. Add to dry ingredients; stir just until blended. Spoon batter into lightly greased mini muffin pans. Bake in a preheated 375° oven for 16 to 18 minutes or until tops are lightly browned. Serve warm.
Yield: about 4 dozen muffins ❄

Butter-Me-Nots

Quick Bean Soup

Cream of Artichoke Soup

- 2 tablespoons olive oil
- 2 tablespoons butter
- 1 cup chopped onion
- 1/2 cup chopped celery
- 2 cans (14 1/2 ounces each) chicken broth
- 2 cans (14 ounces each) artichoke hearts, drained and chopped
- 1 large carrot, sliced
- 2 tablespoons freshly squeezed lemon juice
- 1/2 teaspoon salt
- 1/2 teaspoon ground white pepper
- 1 cup half and half
- 1/4 cup freshly grated Parmesan cheese
  Celery leaves to garnish

In a Dutch oven, combine olive oil and butter over medium heat; stir until butter melts. Sauté onion and celery in oil mixture until onion is translucent. Stir in chicken broth, artichokes, carrot, lemon juice, salt, and white pepper. Cover and cook about 30 minutes or until vegetables are tender. Remove from heat. Purée vegetables in batches in a food processor. Return to Dutch oven. Stir in half and half and cheese. Serve warm or store in an airtight container in refrigerator.

To reheat, cook over medium-low heat uncovered about 20 minutes or until heated through, stirring frequently. Garnish individual servings, if desired.

Yield: about 8 cups soup ✻

Pineapple-Date-Nut Bread

- 3 cups all-purpose flour
- 3/4 cup sugar
- 1 1/2 teaspoons baking powder
- 1/2 teaspoon baking soda
- 1/2 teaspoon salt
- 3/4 cup buttermilk
- 1/3 cup vegetable oil
- 1 egg
- 1 teaspoon vanilla extract
- 1 can (8 ounces) crushed pineapple
- 1 cup chopped dates
- 1 cup chopped walnuts

Grease two 4 1/2" x 8 1/2" baking pans and line with waxed paper. In a large bowl, combine flour, sugar, baking powder, baking soda, and salt. In a small bowl, beat together buttermilk, oil, egg, and vanilla. Stir undrained pineapple into buttermilk mixture. Make a well in dry ingredients; stir in liquid ingredients just until blended. Stir in dates and walnuts. Spoon batter into prepared pans. Bake in a preheated 350° oven for 45 to 55 minutes or until a toothpick inserted in center of bread comes out clean and top is lightly browned. Cool in pans 10 minutes. Serve warm or cool completely on a wire rack.

Yield: 2 loaves bread ✻

Creamy Corn Muffins (recipe on page 104)

Cream of Artichoke Soup

Challah

- ¼ cup sugar
- 2 packages dry yeast
- 2½ cups warm water
- ¾ cup vegetable oil
- ⅓ cup honey
- 2½ teaspoons salt
- ¼ teaspoon ground tumeric
- 4 eggs
- 10 to 10¼ cups all-purpose flour, divided
- Vegetable oil cooking spray
- 2 egg yolks
- 2 teaspoons water
- 4 teaspoons sesame seed

In a medium bowl, dissolve sugar and yeast in 2½ cups warm water. In a large bowl, combine oil, honey, salt, and tumeric. Add 4 eggs and yeast mixture to oil mixture; beat until well blended. Add 9 cups flour; stir until a soft dough forms. Turn dough onto a lightly floured surface. Knead about 5 minutes or until dough becomes smooth and elastic, using additional flour as necessary. Place in a large bowl sprayed with cooking spray, turning once to coat top of dough. Cover and let rise in a warm place (80° to 85°) 1½ hours or until doubled in size.

Turn dough onto a lightly floured surface and punch down. Cover dough and allow to rest 10 minutes. Divide dough into 6 equal pieces. Shape each piece into an 18" rope. For each loaf, braid 3 ropes of dough together; press ends of rope together and tuck under loaf. Transfer to a greased 13½"x16" baking sheet. Spray tops of dough with cooking spray. Cover and let rise in a warm place 1 hour or until doubled in size.

Challah

Pineapple-Date-Nut Bread

Beat egg yolks and 2 teaspoons water together in a small bowl. Brush tops of loaves with egg mixture and sprinkle with sesame seed. Bake in a preheated 375° oven for 25 to 35 minutes or until loaves are golden brown and sound hollow when tapped, alternating position of pans halfway through baking time. Cover with aluminum foil if tops brown too quickly. Serve warm or transfer to a wire rack to cool.
Yield: 2 loaves bread ✳

Cream of Artichoke Soup is versatile—a delicious course for formal dining, or a light meal in itself. Serve it with Creamy Corn Muffins (recipe on page 104). Traditional breads of Christmas include braided Challah and sweet loaves such as Pineapple-Date-Nut Bread.

Burgundy Beef Stew

    3 pounds boneless beef chuck, cut into
        1 1/2" pieces
  1/4 cup vegetable oil
  1/3 cup all-purpose flour
2 1/2 cups red Burgundy wine
2 1/2 cups beef broth
  1/4 cup tomato paste
  3/4 cup finely chopped celery
    5 cloves garlic, minced
    4 bay leaves
    3 teaspoons chopped fresh thyme leaves,
        divided
1 1/4 teaspoons salt
  3/4 teaspoon ground black pepper
    1 pound small potatoes, cut in half
    1 pound baby carrots
    1 pound rutabagas, cut into 1" pieces
    1 pound small onions
    1 package (8 ounces) fresh mushrooms,
        cut in half
  1/4 cup chopped fresh parsley

In an 8-quart Dutch oven, brown small amounts of meat at a time in oil over medium-high heat; set browned meat aside. Reduce heat to medium. Add flour to meat drippings; whisk constantly one minute or until lightly browned. Whisk in wine, beef broth, and tomato paste. Whisking frequently, bring mixture to a boil. Reduce heat to low. Add celery, garlic, bay leaves, 2 teaspoons thyme, salt, pepper, and meat. Cover and simmer 1 3/4 hours or until meat is tender. Add potatoes, carrots, rutabagas, and onions. Bring to a simmer; cover and cook about 45 minutes or until vegetables are tender. Add mushrooms and remaining 1 teaspoon thyme; simmer, uncovered, 10 minutes. Remove bay leaves. Stir in parsley. Serve hot.
Yield: about 16 cups stew ❋

Dill and Green Onion Bread

    1 package dry yeast
    1 cup warm milk
  1/4 cup butter or margarine, softened
  1/4 cup sugar
    1 egg
    2 tablespoons finely chopped fresh dill weed
    2 tablespoons finely chopped green onions
    1 teaspoon salt
3 3/4 to 4 cups all-purpose flour, divided
        Vegetable oil cooking spray
    1 egg
    1 tablespoon water
        Fresh dill sprigs and pieces of green onion
        blades to decorate

In a small bowl, dissolve yeast in warm milk. In a large bowl, combine butter, sugar, 1 egg, chopped dill weed, chopped onions, salt, and yeast mixture; beat until blended. Add 3 3/4 cups flour; stir until a soft dough forms. Turn onto a lightly floured surface and knead about 5 minutes or until dough becomes smooth and elastic, using additional flour as necessary. Place in a large bowl sprayed with cooking spray, turning once to coat top of dough. Cover and let rise in a warm place (80° to 85°) 1 hour or until doubled in size.

Turn dough onto a lightly floured surface and punch down. Divide dough into fourths. Shape into two 4 1/2" round loaves and two 12" long baguette loaves. Place on 2 greased baking sheets. Spray tops of dough with cooking spray, cover, and let rise in a warm place 1 hour or until doubled in size.

In a small bowl, beat remaining egg and water; brush over loaves. Decorate with dill sprigs and green onion blades. Brush decorations with egg mixture. Bake in a preheated 350° oven for 20 to 25 minutes or until bread is golden brown and sounds hollow when tapped. Serve warm or transfer to a wire rack to cool completely. Store in an airtight container.
Yield: 4 loaves bread ❋

Burgundy Beef Stew

Dill and Green Onion Bread

These recipes are hearty winter classics! Burgundy Beef Stew is thick with meat and vegetables long-simmered in a savory broth. Golden-brown and topped with fresh herbs, Dill and Green Onion Bread are the perfect accompaniments.

❄ *main & side dishes* ❄

Christmas dinner entrées can be as casual as spicy Chicken Gumbo (page 116) or as elegant as Châteaubriand with Creamy Caper Sauce. For a meal as memorable as it is delicious, add a variety of original side dishes like Creamed Potatoes or Sugar Snaps with Buttered Pecans.

Châteaubriand with Creamy Caper Sauce

3½ pounds châteaubriand, trimmed of fat
   Olive oil, salt, and ground black pepper
2 teaspoons garlic powder
10 to 12 slices bacon
1 cup water
¼ cup butter or margarine
2 large onions, chopped
3 tablespoons all-purpose flour
1 teaspoon balsamic vinegar
1 teaspoon dried tarragon leaves
¾ cup whipping cream
½ cup dry white wine, divided
1 bottle (3½ ounces) capers, undrained
   Garnish: fresh tarragon

Preheat oven to 400°. Rub beef with oil. Sprinkle salt, pepper, and garlic powder over beef. Wrap bacon around beef, securing with toothpicks. Place beef in a greased 9" x 13" baking pan; pour water into pan. Insert a meat thermometer into center of meat. Place in oven, reduce temperature to 350°, and bake 35 to 40 minutes or until thermometer registers 150° (medium-rare). Remove from oven and keep warm.

For sauce, melt butter in a large skillet over medium heat. Add onions; cook until tender. Stirring occasionally, add flour, vinegar, and dried tarragon; cook 3 minutes. Gradually stir in cream and ¼ cup wine; bring to a boil. Stirring constantly, boil 5 minutes or until thickened. Remove from heat; stir in capers and remaining ¼ cup wine.

To serve, slice meat and remove toothpicks. Spoon sauce over meat and garnish, if desired.
Yield: about 10 servings ❄

Creamed Potatoes

2½ pounds red potatoes, peeled and cut into bite-size pieces
¼ cup butter or margarine
3 tablespoons all-purpose flour
1 teaspoon salt
½ teaspoon ground black pepper
½ teaspoon garlic powder
2 cups milk
   Garnish: melted butter and chopped parsley

Place potatoes in a large saucepan and cover with salted water. Bring to boil and cook until potatoes are tender; drain in a colander.

In same saucepan, melt butter over medium heat. Whisking constantly, add next 4 ingredients and cook 1 minute. Whisking constantly, add milk and cook until thickened. Add potatoes and stir until well coated. Garnish, if desired. Serve warm.
Yield: about 8 servings ❄

Châteaubriand with Creamy Caper Sauce

Creamed Potatoes

Sugar Snaps with Buttered Pecans
(recipe on page 112)

Sugar Snaps with Buttered Pecans

Shown on page 111

- 1/4 cup butter or margarine
- 1/2 cup chopped pecans
- 3 packages (8 ounces each) frozen sugar snap peas, thawed
  Salt
  Ground black pepper

In a medium skillet, melt butter over medium heat. Stirring occasionally, add pecans and cook until pecans are slightly darker in color. Stir in peas and cook until heated through. Salt and pepper to taste. Serve hot.

Yield: about 10 servings ❄

Orange Curried Carrots

- 2 pounds carrots, peeled and sliced
- 1 can (15 ounces) mandarin oranges in light syrup, divided
- 1 1/2 teaspoons salt, divided
- 1/2 teaspoon ground white pepper, divided
- 2 tablespoons butter or margarine
- 1 tablespoon finely minced onion
- 2 tablespoons all-purpose flour
- 1 1/2 teaspoons curry powder
- 1 1/2 cups warm milk
- 1/4 teaspoon ground cinnamon
- 1/8 teaspoon ground ginger
  Garnish: ground cinnamon

Place carrots in a microwave-safe serving dish. Drain oranges, reserving syrup. Pour 1/4 cup reserved mandarin orange syrup over carrots. Sprinkle 1/2 teaspoon salt and 1/4 teaspoon white pepper over carrots. Cover and microwave on HIGH 8 to 12 minutes or until carrots are tender, stirring halfway through cooking. Keep carrots covered while preparing sauce.

Chop oranges into pieces. Melt butter in a heavy medium saucepan over medium heat. Sauté onion in butter until tender. Sprinkle flour and curry powder over butter. Stirring constantly, cook until mixture is well blended and thickened. Gradually add remaining reserved orange syrup and milk; stir until well blended. Stirring constantly, add chopped oranges, remaining 1 teaspoon salt, remaining 1/4 teaspoon white pepper, 1/4 teaspoon cinnamon, and ginger. Cook about 15 minutes or until sauce thickens. Drain carrots; pour sauce over carrots. Garnish, if desired. Serve warm.

Yield: about 10 servings ❄

Lemon-Parsley Asparagus

- 1/2 cup butter, divided
- 1 tablespoon sesame seed
- 1 tablespoon finely minced onion
- 2 tablespoons chopped fresh parsley
- 2 tablespoons freshly squeezed lemon juice
- 1/2 teaspoon grated lemon zest
- 1/2 teaspoon salt
- 1/4 teaspoon ground black pepper
- 2 bunches fresh asparagus spears
  Garnish: lemon zest strips

In a medium skillet, combine 2 tablespoons butter, sesame seed, and onion over medium heat. Stirring frequently, cook until sesame seed is lightly browned and onion is tender. Add remaining 6 tablespoons butter, stirring constantly until butter melts. Remove from heat and stir in chopped parsley, lemon juice, lemon zest, salt, and pepper.

Place asparagus in a microwave-safe serving dish. Cover and microwave on HIGH 3 to 5 minutes or until heated through, rotating dish halfway through cooking time. Pour butter mixture over asparagus. Garnish, if desired. Serve warm.

Yield: 8 to 10 servings ❄

Orange Curried Carrots
Lemon-Parsley Asparagus

Top ordinary vegetables with a citrusy sauce and you get festive flavors
such as Orange Curried Carrots and Lemon-Parsley Asparagus.

Barbecued Turkey

Not your ordinary Christmas dishes—Barbecued Turkey and south-of-the-border Enchiladas with Sweet Red Pepper Sauce are zesty crowd-pleasers!

Barbecued Turkey

- 2 cups chopped onions
- $1/4$ cup vegetable oil
- 2 cloves garlic, minced
- 2 cups ketchup
- $1/2$ cup maple syrup
- $1/2$ cup water
- $1/4$ cup apple cider vinegar
- $1/4$ cup molasses
- $1/4$ cup Worcestershire sauce
- $1/4$ cup Dijon-style mustard
- 1 teaspoon crushed red pepper
- 1 teaspoon celery seed
- 1 teaspoon ground black pepper
- $1/2$ teaspoon ground ginger
- 1 turkey (13 to 15 pounds)
- 2 tablespoons vegetable oil
  Salt and ground black pepper
- 1 cup water
  Garnish: fresh parsley and red and yellow peppers

For sauce, combine onions, $1/4$ cup oil, and garlic in a large saucepan. Cook over medium heat until onions are tender. Stir in next 11 ingredients. Bring to a boil, reduce heat to low, and simmer, uncovered, 30 minutes. Remove from heat.

Remove giblets and neck from turkey. Rinse turkey and pat dry. Rub turkey with 2 tablespoons oil. Liberally salt and pepper turkey inside and out. Tie ends of legs to tail with kitchen twine. Place turkey, breast side up, in a large roasting pan. Insert meat thermometer into thickest part of thigh, making sure thermometer does not touch bone. Pour 1 cup water into pan. Baste turkey with sauce. Loosely cover with aluminum foil and roast in a preheated 350° oven, basting with sauce every 30 minutes, for 3 to $3^1/2$ hours or until meat thermometer registers 180° to 185° and juices run clear when thickest part of thigh is pierced with a fork. Transfer turkey to a serving platter and let stand 20 minutes before carving. Garnish, if desired. Serve warm sauce with turkey.

Yield: 18 to 20 servings ❊

Enchiladas with Sweet Red Pepper Sauce

- 3 sweet red peppers
- $1/2$ cup plus 3 tablespoons finely chopped onion, divided
- 2 cloves garlic, minced
- 2 tablespoons vegetable oil
- 1 can (28 ounces) crushed tomatoes
- 1 can ($14^1/2$ ounces) chicken broth
- $1/2$ teaspoon salt
- $1/2$ teaspoon ground cumin
- $1/4$ teaspoon dried oregano leaves, crushed
- $1^1/2$ pounds ground beef, cooked and drained
- 1 cup sour cream
- 20 corn tortillas (6" dia.)
- 4 cups combined shredded Monterey Jack and Cheddar cheeses, divided

Garnish: chopped fresh cilantro

To roast red peppers, cut in half lengthwise; remove seeds and membranes. Place, skin side up, on an ungreased baking sheet; flatten with hand. Broil about 3" from heat 12 to 15 minutes or until skin is evenly blackened. Immediately seal peppers in a resealable plastic bag and allow to steam 10 to 15 minutes. Remove charred skin. Cut peppers into $1/2$" x 1" strips.

In a heavy large saucepan, sauté $1/2$ cup onion and garlic in oil over medium-high heat until onion is tender. Stir in pepper strips, tomatoes, chicken broth, salt, cumin, and oregano. Bring mixture to a boil. Stirring frequently, reduce heat to medium-low and simmer about 20 minutes or until sauce thickens.

Spread $2/3$ cup sauce in each of 2 greased 7" x 11" baking dishes. In a medium bowl, combine ground beef, remaining 3 tablespoons chopped onion, and sour cream. Soften tortillas in a microwave according to package directions. Place 2 rounded tablespoons ground beef mixture and 2 tablespoons cheese on each tortilla. Tightly roll up tortillas and place 10, seam side down, in each baking dish. Spoon remaining sauce down each side of baking dishes, covering ends of tortillas. Sprinkle remaining cheese over middle of enchiladas. Bake in a preheated 375° oven for 12 to 15 minutes or until heated through and cheese melts. Garnish, if desired. Serve warm.

Yield: 20 enchiladas ❄

Enchiladas with Sweet Red Pepper Sauce

Chicken Gumbo

- 1 chicken (about 4 pounds)
- 2 carrots, quartered
- 1 onion, quartered
- 2 ribs celery with leaves, cut into pieces
- 3 bay leaves
- 3¼ teaspoons salt, divided
- 2 teaspoons ground black pepper, divided
- 12 cups water
- ¾ cup all-purpose flour
- ½ cup vegetable oil
- 2 cups chopped onions
- 2 cups chopped celery
- 1 cup chopped green pepper
- 4 cloves garlic, minced
- 1 package (16 ounces) frozen sliced okra
- 1 can (14½ ounces) diced tomatoes, undrained
- 1 teaspoon dried thyme leaves
- ½ teaspoon ground red pepper
- 1 pound fresh shrimp, cooked, peeled, and deveined
- ¼ cup chopped fresh parsley
- 1½ tablespoons gumbo filé powder
   Hot pepper sauce to taste
   Hot cooked rice to serve

In an 8-quart stockpot, combine chicken, carrots, onion quarters, celery pieces, 1 bay leaf, 2 teaspoons salt, and 1 teaspoon black pepper. Add water. Bring to a boil over high heat. Reduce heat to medium low; cover and simmer about 1 hour or until chicken is tender.

Strain and reserve broth; discard vegetables. Remove meat from chicken and cut into bite-size pieces; set aside.

Stirring constantly, cook flour in hot oil in a large Dutch oven over medium heat 10 minutes or until mixture forms a brown roux. Reduce heat to medium low. Stir in chopped onions, 2 cups celery, green pepper, and garlic. Cook 15 minutes or until vegetables are tender. Stirring constantly, gradually add 6 cups reserved chicken broth. Stir in chicken pieces, okra, tomatoes, remaining 2 bay leaves, thyme, remaining 1¼ teaspoons salt, remaining 1 teaspoon black pepper, and red pepper. Increase heat and bring to a boil. Reduce heat to low; cover and simmer 45 minutes. Stir in shrimp and parsley; cook about 3 minutes or until shrimp are heated through. Stir in filé powder and pepper sauce. Serve hot over rice.

Yield: about 14½ cups gumbo ✻

Chicken Gumbo

Corn Bread Loaf
Cider-Baked Ham

Try one of these regional favorites for Yuletide dining— Chicken Gumbo served over fluffy rice or Cider-Baked Ham with savory Corn Bread Loaf.

Cider-Baked Ham

5 to 6 pound ham
2 cups apple cider, divided
1/4 cup soy sauce
2 tablespoons cornstarch
1 tablespoon water

Place ham in a large roasting pan. Bake in a preheated 450° oven for 30 minutes or until outside is crisp. Remove from oven. Reduce oven temperature to 325°.

In a large bowl, combine 1 1/2 cups cider and soy sauce; pour over ham. Cover with aluminum foil and bake 2 to 3 hours or until meat thermometer registers 185°, basting ham frequently with cider mixture.

For sauce, combine meat drippings and remaining cider in a medium saucepan. In a small bowl, mix together cornstarch and water to make a paste. Spoon into meat drippings, stirring until smooth. Cook over medium heat 10 to 15 minutes or until thick, stirring occassionally. Transfer ham to serving plate and serve with sauce.
Yield: 12 to 16 servings ✼

Corn Bread Loaf

6 tablespoons butter or margarine
1 cup chopped green onions
3/4 cup chopped celery
4 cups corn bread crumbs
4 cups fine plain bread crumbs
10 slices bacon, cooked and crumbled
1 1/2 teaspoons ground sage
3/4 teaspoon salt
1/2 teaspoon ground black pepper
6 eggs, beaten
1 cup chicken broth

In a large skillet, melt butter over medium-high heat. Stir in onions and celery; sauté 8 minutes or until vegetables are tender. In a large bowl, combine bread crumbs. Stir in onion mixture and next 4 ingredients. Stir in eggs and chicken broth. Spoon into a greased and floured 5" x 9" loaf pan. Bake in a preheated 350° oven for 30 to 40 minutes or until top is brown. Unmold onto serving plate and slice. Serve immediately.
Yield: about 10 servings ✼

Zucchini with Basil Butter

1/2 cup butter or margarine
1 cup fresh basil leaves, finely chopped or 2 tablespoons dried basil leaves, crushed
2 pounds zucchini, cut into 2" long strips
1/2 teaspoon salt
1/4 teaspoon ground black pepper

In a large skillet, melt butter over medium heat. Add basil and cook 1 minute if using fresh or 3 minutes if using dried. Add zucchini; cook 3 to 4 minutes longer. Stir in salt and pepper. Serve warm.
Yield: about 8 servings ✲

Potato Croquettes

Shown on page 121

9 medium red potatoes, peeled and quartered (about 3 1/2 pounds)
1/3 cup butter or margarine, softened
1/2 cup finely chopped green onions
3 eggs, beaten
1 teaspoon salt
1/4 teaspoon ground white pepper
1 cup purchased seasoned bread crumbs
  Vegetable oil

In a Dutch oven, cover potatoes with salted water. Bring water to a boil; reduce heat, cover, and cook until potatoes are tender. Drain potatoes. Add butter; beat or mash until potatoes are smooth. Let potatoes cool 20 minutes or until cool enough to handle.

Stir onions, eggs, salt, and white pepper into potatoes. Place bread crumbs on a plate. Spoon about 1/3 cup potato mixture at a time onto bread crumbs and shape into a 3" dia. patty, covering with crumbs.

In a large skillet, heat a small amount of oil. Fry patties in oil until golden brown on both sides, adding oil as needed. Serve warm.
Yield: about 18 potato croquettes ✲

Wild Rice and Cranberry Dressing

1/2 cup butter or margarine
1 1/2 cups chopped onions
3/4 cup thinly sliced celery
2 cloves garlic, minced
1 package (6 ounces) wild rice
1/2 teaspoon dried thyme leaves
1/2 teaspoon dried sage leaves
1/2 teaspoon salt
1/2 teaspoon ground black pepper
3 cans (14 1/2 ounces each) chicken broth
1 package (16 ounces) brown rice
1 package (6 ounces) sweetened dried cranberries
1/2 cup chopped fresh parsley
1 cup coarsely chopped pecans, toasted

In a heavy Dutch oven, melt butter over medium heat. Sauté onions, celery, and garlic until tender. Stir in wild rice, thyme, sage, salt, and pepper. Add chicken broth; bring to a boil. Reduce heat to low; cover and simmer 30 minutes. Stir in brown rice; cover and continue to simmer 30 minutes. Stir in cranberries and parsley; cover and simmer 20 minutes longer or until broth is absorbed. Stir in pecans. Serve warm.
Yield: about 12 cups dressing ✲

Turkey Quiche Lorraine

- 1/2 package (15 ounces) refrigerated pie crust, at room temperature
- 8 slices bacon
- 1/4 cup finely chopped onion
- 1 1/2 cups (about 6 ounces) shredded Gruyère cheese
- 1 cup diced cooked turkey
- 1 1/2 cups half and half
- 4 eggs
- 1/2 teaspoon dry mustard
- 1/4 teaspoon salt

Press pie crust into bottom and up sides of a 9" quiche pan. Flute top edge of crust. Bake crust in a preheated 350° oven for 8 minutes or until lightly browned; set aside.

Cook bacon in a medium skillet until crisp; remove bacon, reserving 1 tablespoon drippings in skillet. Drain and crumble bacon; set aside.

Sauté onion in reserved drippings over medium-low heat until tender. Sprinkle cheese, turkey, bacon, and onion over pie crust. In a medium bowl, beat half and half, eggs, dry mustard, and salt until well blended. Pour egg mixture into pie crust. Bake at 350° for 40 to 50 minutes or until a knife inserted in center of quiche comes out clean. Let stand 5 minutes before serving. Serve warm.

Yield: about 8 servings ✻

Turkey Quiche Lorraine

Turkey Quiche Lorraine puts leftover turkey on your family's list of favorite foods. Refrigerated pie crust shortens preparation time.

A feast for the eyes— Pork Tenderloin with Peach Chutney Glaze is also rich with flavor. Serve it with Potato Croquettes and Red and Green Cabbage Medley for the most satisfying meal of the season.

Pork Tenderloin with Peach Chutney Glaze

Peach Chutney

- 1 cup peach preserves
- 1/2 cup golden raisins
- 1/4 cup chopped pecans
- 2 tablespoons apple cider vinegar
- 2 teaspoons freshly grated ginger
- 1 teaspoon minced onion

Pork Tenderloin

- 1 tablespoon crushed fresh thyme leaves
- 2 cloves garlic, minced
- 2 teaspoons freshly grated ginger
- 1 teaspoon salt
- 1 teaspoon ground black pepper
- 1 pork tenderloin (about 2 pounds)
- Garnish: fresh thyme springs and canned peaches

Pork Tenderloin with Peach Chutney Glaze

For peach chutney, process all ingredients in a food processor until finely chopped. Transfer ingredients to a medium saucepan over low heat. Stirring frequently, cook 7 to 9 minutes or until mixture is heated through. Remove from heat. Cover and allow flavors to blend.

For pork tenderloin, combine thyme, garlic, ginger, salt, and pepper in a small bowl. Rub mixture over pork; place in a roasting pan. Insert meat thermometer into thickest part of tenderloin. Spooning about 1/3 cup chutney over pork after 30 minutes, bake in a preheated 400° oven for 40 to 50 minutes or until meat thermometer registers 160°. Transfer tenderloin to a serving platter and allow to stand 10 minutes before slicing. Garnish, if desired. Serve with remaining peach chutney.

Yield: about 10 servings ❊

Red and Green Cabbage Medley

Red Cabbage

- 2 tablespoons butter or margarine
- 1/4 cup firmly packed brown sugar
- 2 tablespoons cider vinegar
- 1 teaspoon salt
- 1/2 teaspoon ground black pepper
- 13 cups red cabbage, shredded (about a 2-pound cabbage)
- 2 Granny Smith apples, peeled, cored, and thinly sliced
- 1/3 cup finely chopped onion

Green Cabbage

- 5 slices bacon, thinly sliced crosswise
- 1 teaspoon caraway seed
- 1/2 teaspoon salt
- 1/4 teaspoon ground black pepper
- 1 bay leaf
- 13 cups green cabbage, shredded (about a 2-pound cabbage)
- 1/3 cup finely chopped onion
- 1 green pepper, cut into 2" long slivers
- 1/4 cup chicken broth

For red cabbage, melt butter in a large deep skillet over medium-high heat. Stir in brown sugar, vinegar, salt, and pepper. Add cabbage, apples, and onion; stir until well blended. Cover and cook 5 minutes or until cabbage is tender; stirring occasionally.

For green cabbage, cook bacon in a large deep skillet over medium-high heat until crisp. Remove bacon, reserving drippings in skillet. Drain bacon, crumble, and set aside. To drippings, stir in caraway seed, salt, black pepper, and bay leaf. Add cabbage, onion, and green pepper; stir until well blended. Add chicken broth. Cover and cook 5 minutes or until cabbage is tender, stirring occasionally. Remove bay leaf. Stir in bacon. Spoon red and green cabbage into a large bowl. Serve warm.

Yield: 12 to 15 servings each cabbage ❄

Red and Green Cabbage Medley

Potato Croquettes (recipe on page 118)

sweets & desserts

Incredible candies and decadent desserts are on everyone's Christmas wish list, so why not add these amazing recipes to your to-do list? They're worth every minute you spend in the kitchen!

Butterscotch-Pecan Brownies

- $2/3$ cup butter or margarine, softened
- $1^1/2$ cups firmly packed brown sugar
- 2 large eggs
- 2 teaspoons vanilla extract
- 2 cups all-purpose flour
- 1 teaspoon baking powder
- $1/4$ teaspoon baking soda
- 1 teaspoon salt
- 1 cup butterscotch morsels
- $1/2$ cup chopped pecans

Cream butter; add brown sugar, beating well. Add eggs and vanilla to mixture, beating well. Combine flour, baking powder, baking soda, and salt; add to creamed mixture, stirring well. Pour batter into a greased 9" x 13" baking pan. Sprinkle with butterscotch morsels and pecans. Bake in a preheated 350° oven for 30 minutes. Cool; cut into bars.

Yield: about $2^1/2$ dozen bars ❊

Peaches and Cream Soufflés

Soufflés and topping should be made 1 day in advance.

Soufflés

- 8 egg yolks
- 1 cup sugar
- 1 package (16 ounces) frozen unsweetened peaches, thawed and puréed
- 2 tablespoons peach schnapps (optional)
- $1/2$ cup apricot nectar
- 1 package (3 ounces) peach-flavored gelatin
- 1 envelope unflavored gelatin
- 3 cups whipping cream

Topping

- 1 package (16 ounces) frozen unsweetened peaches, thawed and coarsely chopped
- 1 cup sugar
- $1/4$ cup peach schnapps (optional)

For soufflés, beat egg yolks and sugar until creamy in a medium bowl using an electric mixer. Stir in peaches. If desired, stir in schnapps. In a large saucepan, combine apricot nectar and gelatins. Cook over low heat, stirring until gelatins dissolve. Stir peach mixture into gelatin mixture, mixing well. Stirring constantly, cook over medium heat until mixture begins to boil. Remove from heat and cool to room temperature.

Place a large bowl and beaters from an electric mixer in refrigerator until well chilled. In chilled bowl, whip cream until stiff. Fold whipped cream into peach mixture. Spoon into 4-ounce ramekins, filling each $3/4$ full. Cover and refrigerate until firm.

For topping, combine peaches and sugar in a medium saucepan; bring to a boil. Cook about 15 minutes or until sauce thickens slightly. Remove from heat. If desired, stir in schnapps. Cover and refrigerate until chilled. To serve, spoon about 1 tablespoon topping over each soufflé.

Yield: about 18 soufflés ❊

Almond-Poppy Seed Angel Food Cake

Mocha Pudding Cake

Almond-Poppy Seed Angel Food Cake

- 1 package (16 ounces) angel food cake mix and ingredients to prepare cake
- 2 tablespoons poppy seed
- 1½ teaspoons almond extract, divided
- 1½ cups confectioners sugar
- 2 tablespoons water
- ¼ cup sliced almonds

Prepare cake mix according to package directions, stirring in poppy seed and 1 teaspoon almond extract. Pour into an ungreased 10" tube pan. Bake in a preheated 350° oven for 40 to 45 minutes or until top is golden brown. Invert pan; cool completely.

Transfer cake to a serving plate. Combine confectioners sugar, water, and remaining ½ teaspoon almond extract in a small bowl. Drizzle glaze over cake; sprinkle with almonds.

Yield: 16 servings ❄

Cake mix makes it easy to create the Almond-Poppy Seed Angel Food Cake. Melt-in-your-mouth Mocha Pudding Cake will please any chocolate lover, while can't-fail Grasshopper Pie is refreshing with creamy mint.

Mocha Pudding Cake

- 1 cup all-purpose flour
- 3/4 cup granulated sugar
- 1/4 cup plus 2 tablespoons cocoa, divided
- 1 1/2 teaspoons baking powder
- 1/4 teaspoon salt
- 1/2 cup milk
- 2 tablespoons vegetable oil
- 1 teaspoon vanilla extract
- 1 cup firmly packed brown sugar
- 1 3/4 cups boiling strongly-brewed coffee
- 9 tablespoons frozen whipped topping, thawed

Combine flour, granulated sugar, 2 tablespoons cocoa, baking powder, and salt in a 9" square baking pan. Add milk, oil, and vanilla; whisk until smooth. In a small bowl, combine brown sugar and remaining 1/4 cup cocoa; sprinkle over batter. Pour coffee over batter (do not stir). Bake in a preheated 350° oven for 40 to 45 minutes or until a toothpick inserted in cake portion comes out clean. Cool cake in pan 5 minutes. Top each serving with 1 tablespoon whipped topping.

Yield: about 9 servings ✳

Grasshopper Pie

Grasshopper Pie

Crust

- 30 chocolate wafer cookies
- 1/4 cup butter or margarine, melted

Filling

- 30 large marshmallows
- 1/2 cup milk
- 1/4 cup crème de menthe
- 1 cup whipping cream
  Green liquid food coloring (optional)
  Garnish: 16 chocolate mint wafer candies

For crust, finely grind cookies in a food processor. With food processor running, slowly add melted butter; process until well blended. Press crumb mixture into bottom and up sides of a 9" pie pan. Bake crust in a preheated 350° oven for 7 minutes. Cool completely on a wire rack.

For filling, place a medium bowl and beaters from an electric mixer in refrigerator until well chilled. In the top of a double boiler, combine marshmallows and milk. Stirring frequently, cook over hot, not boiling, water until mixture is smooth. Remove from heat and pour into a large bowl. Cool to room temperature. Stir in crème de menthe.

In chilled bowl, whip cream until soft peaks form. Fold whipped cream into marshmallow mixture. If desired, tint green. Spoon evenly into cooled crust. Loosely cover and refrigerate until set. Garnish, if desired.

Yield: about 8 servings ✳

Pinecone Cookies

Cookies

- $3/4$ cup butter or margarine, softened
- $1/2$ cup sugar
- 1 egg
- 1 tablespoon freshly squeezed lemon juice
- $1/2$ teaspoon grated lemon zest
- $1/2$ teaspoon vanilla extract
- $1 3/4$ cups all-purpose flour
- $1/4$ teaspoon salt

Icing

- 4 cups confectioners sugar
- 2 tablespoons plus 2 teaspoons water
- 2 tablespoons freshly squeezed lemon juice
- $1/2$ teaspoon grated lemon zest
- $1/2$ teaspoon vanilla extract
- $1 1/2$ cups sliced almonds, toasted

For cookies, cream butter and sugar in a large bowl until fluffy. Add egg, lemon juice, lemon zest, and vanilla; beat until smooth. In a small bowl, combine flour and salt. Add dry ingredients to creamed mixture; stir until a soft dough forms. Divide dough in half. Wrap in plastic wrap and chill 2 hours or until dough is firm enough to handle.

On a lightly floured surface, use a floured rolling pin to roll out dough to $1/4$" thickness. Use a $2 1/2$" wide x $3 1/2$" long oval scalloped-edge cookie cutter to cut out cookies. Transfer to a greased baking sheet. Bake in a preheated 375° oven for 8 to 10 minutes or until bottoms are lightly browned. Transfer cookies to a wire rack to cool.

For icing, combine confectioners sugar, water, lemon juice, lemon zest, and vanilla in a medium bowl; beat until smooth. Working with 3 cookies at a time, spread icing on cookies. Before icing hardens, place almonds on cookies to resemble pinecones. Let icing harden. Store in a single layer in an airtight container.

Yield: about 2 dozen cookies ❅

Hazelnut Coffee Cake

Cake

- 1 cup butter or margarine, softened
- $1 1/3$ cups granulated sugar
- 3 eggs
- $1 1/2$ teaspoons vanilla extract
- $2 1/2$ cups sifted cake flour
- 1 teaspoon baking powder
- 1 teaspoon baking soda
- $1/8$ teaspoon salt
- $1 1/3$ cups sour cream
- $1 1/4$ cups chopped hazelnuts, toasted
- $1/2$ cup firmly packed brown sugar
- 1 teaspoon ground cinnamon

Icing

- 2 squares (1 ounce each) bittersweet baking chocolate
- 4 teaspoons hazelnut-flavored liqueur
- 1 tablespoon light corn syrup

For cake, cream butter and granulated sugar in a large bowl until fluffy. Add eggs and vanilla; beat until smooth. In a medium bowl, combine cake flour, baking powder, baking soda, and salt. Alternately beat dry ingredients and sour cream into creamed mixture, beating just until blended. Spoon $1/3$ of batter into bottom of a greased and floured 9" springform pan with a tube insert. In a small bowl, combine hazelnuts, brown sugar, and cinnamon. Sprinkle $1/3$ of hazelnut mixture over batter. Continue layering batter and hazelnut mixture, ending with hazelnut mixture. Bake in a preheated 325° oven for 55 to 65 minutes or until a toothpick inserted in center of cake comes out clean. Cool cake in pan on a wire rack 10 minutes. Run a knife around edge of pan; remove sides of pan. Cool completely. Carefully remove bottom of pan; transfer cake to a serving plate.

For icing, place chocolate, liqueur, and corn syrup in the top of a double boiler over hot water. Stirring frequently, cook until chocolate melts and mixture is smooth. Drizzle chocolate mixture over cake. Store in an airtight container.

Yield: about 16 servings ❅

Nut lovers will rave about Pinecone Cookies and Hazelnut Coffee Cake! If you enjoy the traditional flavors of Christmas, treat yourself to Marlborough Pie. The cinnamon-custard filling is packed full of tart apple bits and enhanced by a splash of cream sherry.

Hazelnut Coffee Cake
Marlborough Pie
Pinecone Cookies

Marlborough Pie

    4   eggs
    1   cup sugar
    1   cup whipping cream
  ¹/₄   cup cream sherry
    1   tablespoon butter, melted
  ¹/₂   teaspoon ground cinnamon
  ¹/₈   teaspoon salt
    2   cups unpeeled, cored, and finely chopped
        Granny Smith apples
    1   unbaked 9" pie crust

In a medium bowl, beat eggs and sugar until smooth. Add whipping cream, sherry, melted butter, cinnamon, and salt; beat until well blended. Stir in apples. Pour into crust. Bake in a preheated 400° oven for 10 minutes. Reduce temperature to 350°. Bake for 40 to 50 minutes or until center is firm. Let stand 1¹/₂ hours before serving. Store in an airtight container in refrigerator.
Yield: about 8 servings ❄

Put a fluffy new topping on a holiday classic by making Sweet Potato Pie with Marshmallow Meringue. Guests will feel truly special if you serve elegant Bananas Foster Crêpes.

Sweet Potato Pie with Marshmallow Meringue

Sweet Potato Pie with Marshmallow Meringue

Spoon meringue onto hot pie for best results.

Pie
- 1 can (29 ounces) sweet potatoes in syrup, drained and mashed
- 1 cup firmly packed brown sugar
- 2 tablespoons butter or margarine, softened
- 3 egg yolks
- 1 teaspoon pumpkin pie spice
- 1 teaspoon vanilla extract
- 1/4 teaspoon salt
- 1 can (5 ounces) evaporated milk
- 1 unbaked 9" deep-dish pie crust

Meringue
- 1/2 cup water
- 2 tablespoons sugar
- 1 tablespoon cornstarch
- 1/8 teaspoon salt
- 3 egg whites
- 1/4 teaspoon cream of tartar
- 1 jar (7 ounces) marshmallow creme
- 1/2 teaspoon vanilla extract

For pie, combine sweet potatoes, brown sugar, butter, egg yolks, pumpkin pie spice, vanilla, and salt in a medium bowl; beat until well blended. Stir in evaporated milk. Pour mixture into crust. Bake in a preheated 400° oven for 10 minutes. Reduce heat to 350°. Bake 40 minutes or until center is almost set and edges are cracked and lightly browned.

About 25 minutes after placing pie in oven, combine water, sugar, cornstarch, and salt in a small saucepan for meringue. Stirring constantly, cook over medium heat about 5 minutes or until mixture is clear. Transfer to a heatproof bowl. Cool about 15 minutes.

In a medium bowl, beat egg whites and cream of tartar until foamy. Add cornstarch mixture; beat until well blended. Gradually add marshmallow creme and vanilla; beat until soft peaks form. Top hot pie with meringue, sealing edges to crust; return pie to oven. Bake 12 to 15 minutes or until meringue is lightly browned. Let stand 30 minutes; serve warm.

Yield: about 8 servings ❊

Bananas Foster Crêpes

Crêpes
- ¾ cup milk
- ½ cup all-purpose flour
- 1 egg
- 1 tablespoon granulated sugar
- 2 teaspoons vegetable oil
- ⅛ teaspoon salt

Filling
- 4 ripe bananas
  Lemon juice
- ⅔ cup firmly packed brown sugar
- 6 tablespoons butter or margarine
- ½ teaspoon ground cinnamon
- ¼ cup banana liqueur
- ¼ cup rum
  Vanilla ice cream to serve

For crêpes, combine all ingredients in a medium bowl; beat until smooth. Heat a lightly greased 8" skillet over medium heat. Spoon about 2 tablespoons batter into skillet. Tilt skillet to spread batter evenly in bottom of pan to form a 5½" circle. Cook until edges are light brown; remove from skillet. Repeat with remaining batter. Separate crêpes with waxed paper. (If making in advance, cover and refrigerate; bring to room temperature before serving.)

For filling, peel bananas. Cut each banana in half crosswise and in half again lengthwise. Brush with lemon juice. In a large skillet, combine sugar, butter, and cinnamon. Stirring constantly, cook over medium heat until sugar dissolves. Add bananas; cook 3 to 4 minutes, turning once. Pour liqueur and rum over bananas and cook 2 minutes longer. Remove from heat. Reserving sauce, place 2 banana slices on each crêpe. Fold edges of crêpe over bananas; place on serving plate. Spoon reserved sauce over crêpes. Serve immediately with ice cream.

Yield: 8 servings ❊

Bananas Foster Crêpes

Orange Black Bottom Pie is a unique dessert with layers of chocolate fudge and creamy orange gelatin. Because of the pudding mix added to the batter, Holiday Cherry Cakes are extra-moist.

Orange Black Bottom Pie

Orange Black Bottom Pie

Crust

1½ cups all-purpose flour
½ teaspoon salt
½ cup vegetable shortening
¼ cup cold water

Filling

¾ cup whipping cream, divided
½ cup semisweet chocolate chips
2 tablespoons butter or margarine
2 teaspoons orange extract, divided
1 cup water
1 package (3 ounces) orange-flavored gelatin
1 package (8 ounces) cream cheese, softened
1 cup confectioners sugar, sifted

Decorative Topping

2 tablespoons water
2 tablespoons granulated sugar
1½ teaspoons unflavored gelatin
½ cup whipping cream

For crust, sift flour and salt together in a medium bowl. Using a pastry blender or 2 knives, cut in shortening until mixture resembles coarse meal. Sprinkle with water; mix until a soft dough forms. On a lightly floured surface, use a floured rolling pin to roll out dough to ⅛" thickness. Cut out a 13" circle. Press dough into bottom and up sides of a 9" deep-dish pie plate; fold edges of dough under and flute. Prick bottom of crust with a fork. Bake in a preheated 450° oven for 12 to 15 minutes or until light brown. Cool completely on a wire rack.

For filling, combine ¼ cup whipping cream, chocolate chips, and butter in a small saucepan. Stirring constantly, cook over low heat until smooth. Stir in 1 teaspoon orange extract. Pour into cooled crust.

Chill medium bowl and beaters from an electric mixer in freezer. In a medium saucepan, bring water to a boil. Add orange-flavored gelatin; stir until dissolved. Remove from heat; cool to room temperature.

In a large bowl, beat cream cheese, confectioners sugar, and remaining 1 teaspoon orange extract until fluffy. Beat gelatin mixture into cream cheese mixture. In chilled bowl, whip remaining ½ cup whipping cream until stiff peaks form. Fold whipped cream into cream cheese mixture. Return a clean bowl and beaters to freezer. Pour filling evenly over chocolate mixture. Cover and refrigerate until pie is set.

For decorative topping, combine water, sugar, and gelatin in a small saucepan; let stand 1 minute. Stirring constantly, cook over low heat until gelatin and sugar dissolve. Remove from heat. In chilled bowl, beat whipping cream until soft peaks form. Add sugar mixture and beat until stiff peaks form. Transfer topping to a pastry bag fitted with a large star tip. Pipe a decorative border along top edge of pie. Cover and refrigerate until ready to serve.
Yield: about 8 servings ❋

Holiday Cherry Cakes

1 package (18¼ ounces) cherry chip cake mix
1 package (3.4 ounces) vanilla instant pudding mix
4 eggs
1 cup water
⅓ cup vegetable oil
2 containers (4 ounces each) red candied cherries, chopped
4½ to 4¾ cups confectioners sugar
7 tablespoons milk
3 tablespoons vegetable shortening
2 tablespoons light corn syrup
1 teaspoon clear vanilla extract
1 tube each green and red decorating icing

In a large bowl, combine cake mix, pudding mix, eggs, water, and oil; beat 2 minutes or until smooth. Stir in cherries. Spoon ½ cup batter into each greased mold of a 6-mold fluted tube pan. Bake in a preheated 350° oven for 20 to 23 minutes or until a toothpick inserted in center of cake comes out clean. Cool in pan 5 minutes. Remove from pan and cool completely on a wire rack.

In a large bowl, combine confectioners sugar, milk, shortening, corn syrup, and vanilla; beat until smooth. Spoon white icing over tops of cakes; let icing harden. Transfer red and green icing into pastry bags. Use green icing and a small leaf tip to pipe holly leaves onto cakes. Use red icing and a small round tip to pipe berries onto cakes; let icing harden.
Yield: about 2 dozen cakes ❋

Holiday Cherry Cakes

Apple Streusel Pie

Crust

- ³/₄ cup sifted cake flour
- ¹/₂ teaspoon sugar
- ¹/₈ teaspoon salt
- ¹/₈ teaspoon baking powder
- 2 tablespoons chilled margarine, cut into pieces
- 2 tablespoons cold water
  Vegetable oil cooking spray

Filling

- ³/₄ cup sugar
- 2 tablespoons all-purpose flour
- 1 teaspoon ground cinnamon
- ¹/₄ teaspoon ground nutmeg
- 5 cups peeled, cored, and sliced baking apples (about 4 large apples)

Topping

- ¹/₃ cup quick-cooking oats
- 2 tablespoons sugar
- 2 tablespoons all-purpose flour
- 2 tablespoons chilled margarine, cut into pieces

For crust, combine cake flour, sugar, salt, and baking powder in a small bowl. Using a pastry blender or 2 knives, cut in margarine until mixture resembles coarse meal. Sprinkle with water; stir with a fork until moistened. Shape dough into a ball and place between 2 sheets of plastic wrap. Roll out dough into a 12" circle. Remove top sheet of plastic wrap. Invert dough into a 9" pie plate sprayed with cooking spray. Remove remaining sheet of plastic wrap. Fold edges of dough under and flute. Prick bottom of crust with a fork. Bake in a preheated 400° oven for 8 minutes; set aside.

Reduce oven temperature to 375°. For filling, combine sugar, flour, cinnamon, and nutmeg in a large bowl. Stir in apples. Spoon apple mixture into crust. Bake 25 minutes.

For topping, combine oats, sugar, and flour in a small bowl; cut in margarine with a fork until mixture is crumbly. Sprinkle over pie; bake 45 to 55 minutes or until topping is lightly browned. If crust is browning too quickly, cover edges with aluminum foil. Cool 1 hour before serving.

Yield: about 8 servings ✺

Apple Streusel Pie

Braided Candy Canes

3/4 cup butter or margarine, softened
1 cup sugar
3 eggs
1 tablespoon vanilla extract
4 cups all-purpose flour
1 tablespoon baking powder
1/2 teaspoon baking soda
Vegetable oil cooking spray
Red sugar crystals

Beat butter at medium speed with an electric mixer until soft and creamy; gradually add sugar, beating well. Add eggs and vanilla, mixing well. Combine flour, baking powder, and baking soda; gradually add flour mixture to butter mixture, mixing at low speed just until blended. Divide dough into fourths. Divide each fourth of dough into 14 portions. Roll each portion into an 8" rope; place two ropes together and twist. Shape twists into candy canes, lightly coat with cooking spray, and sprinkle with sugar crystals. Place cookies 2" apart on lightly greased baking sheets; bake in a preheated 350° oven for 10 to 12 minutes or until the edges begin to brown. Transfer to wire racks to cool.
Yield: 28 cookies ❊

Braided Candy Canes

The aromas of cinnamon and nutmeg will fill the house as you bake Apple Streusel Pie. The recipe for Braided Candy Canes is so simple, you'll want to make additional batches for all your friends!

Coconut Fruitcake Bars

Crust

- 12 ounces fruitcake, cut into pieces
- 1/3 cup old-fashioned oats
- 1/3 cup sweetened flaked coconut

Filling

- 1 cup firmly packed brown sugar
- 2 teaspoons all-purpose flour
- 1/2 teaspoon baking powder
- 1/4 teaspoon salt
- 2 eggs
- 1 teaspoon vanilla extract
- 1 1/2 cups sweetened flaked coconut
- 1 cup chopped pecans, divided

Line a greased 9" square baking pan with aluminum foil, extending foil over 2 sides of pan; grease foil. For crust, process fruitcake, oats, and coconut in a food processor until well blended. Press mixture into prepared pan.

For filling, combine brown sugar, flour, baking powder, and salt in a medium bowl. Beat in eggs and vanilla until well blended. Stir in coconut and 1/2 cup pecans. Pour filling over crust. Sprinkle remaining 1/2 cup pecans over filling. Bake in a preheated 350° oven for 20 to 25 minutes or until almost set in center and golden brown. Cool in pan on a wire rack. Lift from pan using ends of foil. Cut into 1" x 2" bars.

Yield: about 2 1/2 dozen bars ❋

What do you do with leftover fruitcake or cinnamon rolls? Make scrumptious Coconut Fruitcake Bars or Cinnamon Roll Bread Pudding! These recipes are wonderful ways to continue enjoying the flavors of the season.

Cinnamon Roll Bread Pudding

Bread Pudding

- 12 to 16 large day-old cinnamon rolls, torn into small pieces (about 12 cups)
- 1/3 cup raisins
- 1/3 cup chopped pecans
- 1 quart milk
- 5 eggs
- 1 cup sugar
- 1 teaspoon vanilla extract
- 1/4 cup butter or margarine, sliced

Vanilla Sauce

- 1 1/3 cups whipping cream
- 1/2 cup sugar, divided
- 4 egg yolks
- 1 teaspoon vanilla extract

For bread pudding, place cinnamon roll pieces in a greased 9" x 13" baking dish. Sprinkle raisins and pecans over rolls. In a large bowl, beat milk, eggs, sugar, and vanilla until well blended; pour over rolls. Cover and chill overnight.

Dot mixture with butter slices. Place dish in a roasting pan; fill pan with hot water halfway up sides of baking dish. Bake in a preheated 350° oven for 40 to 45 minutes or until bread pudding is set in center.

For vanilla sauce, heat whipping cream and 1/4 cup sugar in the top of a double boiler over simmering water. Combine egg yolks and remaining 1/4 cup sugar in a small bowl; beat until well blended. Stir some of hot cream mixture into egg mixture; return egg mixture to double boiler. Stirring constantly, cook 8 to 10 minutes or until mixture thickens slightly and coats a spoon. Remove from heat; stir in vanilla. Serve warm sauce over bread pudding.

Yield: about 15 servings ❋

Coconut Fruitcake Bars

Cinnamon Roll Bread Pudding

So delicious with a cup of cocoa or coffee, White or Dark Chocolate Dreams are sweet squares of old-fashioned shortbread. Surprise the household with another timeless treat—Cranberry-Apple Turnovers. Frozen puff pastry cuts the preparation time in half!

White or Dark Chocolate Dreams

White or Dark Chocolate Dreams

- ³/₄ cup shortening
- ³/₄ cup butter, softened
- 2¹/₄ cups sugar
- 3 large eggs
- 1¹/₂ teaspoons vanilla extract
- 6 ounces white or semisweet chocolate, melted and cooled
- 5³/₄ cups all-purpose flour
- 2¹/₄ teaspoons baking powder
- 1¹/₂ teaspoons salt

Beat shortening and butter at medium speed with an electric mixer until creamy; gradually add sugar, beating well. Add eggs and vanilla, beating until blended. Stir in melted chocolate. Combine flour, baking powder, and salt. Add flour mixture to butter mixture, beating at low speed until thoroughly combined. Divide dough into fourths; chill 1 hour.

Working with ¹/₄ of the dough at a time, roll to ¹/₄" thickness with a lightly floured rolling pin on lightly greased aluminum foil, or cover dough with plastic wrap and roll out. Transfer aluminum foil with dough to a baking sheet. Make horizontal and vertical cuts in dough every 2", using a pizza cutter. Do not remove dough squares; only remove excess dough along edges. Bake in a preheated 350° oven for 10 to 12 minutes or until bottom of cookies are golden brown. Cool on baking sheets 2 minutes; recut using pizza cutter. Transfer to wire racks to cool.

Yield: about 7 dozen cookies ✳

Cranberry-Apple Turnovers

Turnovers

$2^1/_2$ cups peeled, cored, and chopped tart cooking apples (about 3 apples)
$^3/_4$ cup fresh cranberries
1   cup granulated sugar
$^1/_4$ cup chopped walnuts
2   tablespoons all-purpose flour
$^1/_2$ teaspoon ground cinnamon
$^1/_4$ teaspoon ground nutmeg
2   sheets (one $17^1/_4$-ounce package) frozen puff pastry dough, thawed according to package directions

Glaze

$^1/_2$ cup confectioners sugar
2   teaspoons milk

Cranberry-Apple Turnovers

For turnovers, combine apples, cranberries, granulated sugar, walnuts, flour, cinnamon, and nutmeg in a large saucepan. Stirring occasionally, bring to a boil over medium heat. Reduce heat, cover, and simmer about 5 minutes or until apples are tender. Remove from heat.

On a lightly floured surface, cut each sheet of pastry into fourths. Spoon about $^1/_4$ cup apple mixture into center of each pastry square. Fold dough in half diagonally over filling to form a triangle; use a fork to crimp edges together. Place on a greased baking sheet. Bake in a preheated 400° oven for 16 to 18 minutes or until golden brown.

For glaze, combine confectioners sugar and milk in a small bowl; stir until smooth. Drizzle glaze over warm turnovers. Serve warm or at room temperature.
Yield: 8 servings ❅

Peanut Butter Balls

$1^1/_4$ cups smooth peanut butter
$^2/_3$ cup butter or margarine, softened
1   teaspoon vanilla extract
1   package (16 ounces) confectioners sugar
8   ounces chocolate candy coating
1   package (6 ounces) semisweet chocolate chips
    Chocolate sprinkles

In a large bowl, beat peanut butter, butter, and vanilla until well blended. Gradually beat in confectioners sugar. Shape mixture into 1" balls and place on a baking sheet lined with waxed paper. Chill 45 minutes or until firm.

In the top of a double boiler, melt candy coating and chocolate chips over hot water. Dip peanut butter balls into melted chocolate. Return to baking sheet; sprinkle with chocolate sprinkles. Chill until chocolate hardens. Store in an airtight container in refrigerator.
Yield: about $6^1/_2$ dozen candies ❅

Special Pumpkin Pie

1 frozen 9" (2 pounds, 5 ounces) deep-dish pumpkin pie
2 packages (3 ounces each) cream cheese, softened
1/4 cup confectioners sugar
1/4 cup sour cream
1 tablespoon rum or 2 teaspoons rum extract
1/2 teaspoon vanilla extract
   Garnish: toasted walnut halves

Bake pumpkin pie according to package directions; cool. Cover and chill overnight.

In a small bowl, beat cream cheese and confectioners sugar until fluffy. Add sour cream, rum, and vanilla; beat until smooth. Spread topping over chilled pie. Garnish, if desired. Store in an airtight container in refrigerator.
Yield: about 8 servings ❋

Almond Pound Cakes

1 cup butter or margarine, softened
1 1/2 cups sugar
4 eggs
2 teaspoons almond extract
2 cups all-purpose flour
1 teaspoon baking powder
1/2 teaspoon salt
1/2 cup milk

Grease and flour four 3 1/4" x 5 3/4" loaf pans. In a large bowl, cream butter and sugar until fluffy. Add eggs, 1 at a time, beating well after each addition. Beat in almond extract. In a small bowl, combine flour, baking powder, and salt. Alternately beat dry ingredients and milk into creamed mixture, beating until well blended. Spread batter into prepared pans. Bake in a preheated 350° oven for 33 to 37 minutes or until a toothpick inserted in center of cake comes out clean. Cool in pans 10 minutes. Remove from pans and cool completely on a wire rack. Store in an airtight container.
Yield: 4 cakes ❋

Double Chocolate Dream Brownies

16 squares (1 ounce each) semisweet baking chocolate, chopped
1 cup butter or margarine, cut into pieces
1/3 cup strongly brewed coffee
1 1/2 cups sugar
4 eggs
1 teaspoon vanilla extract
1/2 cup all-purpose flour
1 cup chopped walnuts
1 package (6 ounces) white baking chocolate, coarsely chopped

Line a 9" x 13" baking pan with aluminum foil, extending foil over ends of pan; grease foil. In the top of a double boiler, combine semisweet chocolate, butter, and coffee. Stirring frequently, cook over hot, not simmering, water until chocolate melts. Remove from heat; cool 15 minutes.

Place sugar in a large bowl. Add eggs, 1 at a time, beating well after each addition. Beat in vanilla. Gradually stir in cooled chocolate mixture and flour just until blended. Stir in walnuts and white chocolate. Pour into prepared pan. Bake in a preheated 375° oven for 25 to 30 minutes or until center is set. Cool in pan on a wire rack. Cover and chill overnight.

Use ends of foil to lift brownies from pan. Cut into 1" squares. Store in an airtight container in refrigerator.
Yield: about 7 dozen brownies ❋

Since it starts with a frozen pie, Special Pumpkin Pie is a snap to prepare—just mix the cream cheese topping and spread it on the baked and chilled pie. Almond Pound Cakes offer just a touch of sweetness, while Double Chocolate Dream Brownies are everything their name implies.

Special Pumpkin Pie
Double Chocolate Dream Brownies
Almond Pound Cakes

139

Peanut Butter Crème Caramel
Peppermint Cheesecake Squares

Peanut Butter Crème Caramel

1¼ cups sugar, divided
¼ cup water
¼ teaspoon cream of tartar
2¼ cups 2% milk
¼ cup reduced-calorie smooth peanut butter
1¼ cups nonfat egg substitute

In a small saucepan, combine ¾ cup sugar, water, and cream of tartar. Stirring constantly, cook over medium-low heat until sugar dissolves. Increase heat to medium and bring mixture to a boil. Without stirring, cook 10 to 15 minutes or until mixture is a deep golden brown. Remove from heat and immediately pour mixture into an 8" round cake pan, tilting to evenly coat bottom.

Combine milk and peanut butter in a medium saucepan. Whisking constantly, cook over medium heat until smooth and heated through; remove from heat. Combine egg substitute and remaining ½ cup sugar in a medium bowl; whisk until well blended. Gradually add milk mixture to egg mixture, stirring well. Pour mixture over caramelized sugar in cake pan. Place in a 9" x 13" baking pan. Add hot water to baking pan to come halfway up sides of cake pan. Bake in a preheated 325° oven for 1 hour or until a knife inserted in center comes out clean. Transfer cake pan to a wire rack to cool. Cover and chill overnight. Unmold onto a serving plate.
Yield: about 12 servings ✽

Peanut Butter Crème Caramel and Peppermint Cheesecake Squares are made with reduced-calorie and nonfat ingredients, yet both are still rich and creamy. The recipe for Macadamia Nut Fudge Tart gets the heavenly flavor of mocha from cocoa, coffee, and coffee-liqueur.

Peppermint Cheesecake Squares

Crust

- 2/3 cup graham cracker crumbs
- 1 1/2 tablespoons sugar
- 1 tablespoon reduced-calorie margarine, softened
- Vegetable oil cooking spray

Cheesecake

- 12 ounces Neufchâtel cheese, softened
- 1 cup nonfat cottage cheese
- 1/2 cup sugar
- 2 tablespoons white crème de menthe
- 1 teaspoon vanilla extract
- 3/4 cup nonfat egg substitute
- 1/2 cup crushed peppermint candies

For crust, combine cracker crumbs, sugar, and margarine in a small bowl. Press crumb mixture evenly into bottom of a 7" x11" baking dish sprayed with cooking spray. Bake in a preheated 350° oven for 5 minutes. Cool on a wire rack.

For cheesecake, process Neufchâtel cheese, cottage cheese, sugar, crème de menthe, and vanilla in a food processor until smooth. Add egg substitute; process just until blended. Pour batter over crust. Bake in a preheated 350° oven for 25 to 28 minutes or until mixture is almost set. Cool 45 minutes on a wire rack. Cover and chill 6 hours.

To serve, sprinkle crushed candies over cheesecake. Cut into 2" squares. Serve immediately.

Yield: about 15 servings ❋

Macadamia Nut Fudge Tart

Crust

- 1 3/4 cups all-purpose flour
- 1/3 cup cocoa
- 1/4 cup sugar
- 1/8 teaspoon salt
- 3/4 cup butter or margarine, chilled and cut into pieces
- 1/2 cup strongly brewed coffee, chilled

Filling

- 1 package (6 ounces) semisweet chocolate chips, melted
- 2/3 cup sugar
- 2 tablespoons butter or margarine, melted
- 2 tablespoons milk
- 2 teaspoons coffee-flavored liqueur
- 2 eggs, beaten
- 1/2 cup chopped macadamia nuts

For crust, combine first 4 ingredients in a large bowl. Using a pastry blender or 2 knives, cut butter into dry ingredients until mixture resembles coarse meal. Add coffee and knead until a soft dough forms. Cover and chill 8 hours or overnight.

On a lightly floured surface, use a floured rolling pin to roll out dough to an 11" circle. Press into a greased 9" round tart pan. Chill at least 1 hour.

For filling, combine first 5 ingredients in a large bowl. Add eggs, beating until smooth. Fold in nuts. Pour filling into tart crust. Bake in a preheated 350° oven for 30 to 40 minutes or until top is dry and firm (inside will be soft). Cool completely in pan.

Yield: about 16 servings ❋

Macadamia Nut Fudge Tart

Chocolate-Banana
Cream Pie

A new flavor combination for the holidays—Chocolate-Banana Cream Pie chilled under a layer of meringue. A quick recipe for a party snack, Chocolate-Mint Cheese Ball has only four ingredients.

Chocolate-Banana Cream Pie

Crust
- 3/4 cup sifted cake flour
- 1/2 teaspoon sugar
- 1/8 teaspoon salt
- 1/8 teaspoon baking powder
- 2 tablespoons chilled margarine, cut into pieces
- 2 tablespoons cold water
- Vegetable oil cooking spray

Meringue
- 3 egg whites
- 1/4 teaspoon cream of tartar
- 6 tablespoons sugar

Filling
- 1 egg
- 1 egg yolk
- 1/2 cup sugar
- 3 tablespoons cornstarch
- 1/8 teaspoon salt
- 1 1/2 cups skim milk
- 1/2 teaspoon vanilla extract
- 1 square (1 ounce) semisweet baking chocolate, chopped
- 1 banana, sliced

For crust, combine cake flour, sugar, salt, and baking powder in a medium bowl. Using a pastry blender or 2 knives, cut in margarine until mixture resembles coarse meal. Sprinkle with water; stir with a fork until moistened. Shape dough into a ball and place between 2 sheets of plastic wrap. Roll out dough into a 12" circle. Invert dough into a 9" pie plate sprayed with cooking spray. Flute edges of dough. Prick bottom of crust with fork. Bake in a preheated 400° oven for 12 minutes; cool completely.

Reduce oven temperature to 350°. For meringue, beat egg whites at high speed of an electric mixer until foamy. Add cream of tartar; beat until soft peaks form. Add sugar, 1 tablespoon at a time, beating until sugar dissolves and stiff peaks form. Set meringue aside.

For filling, beat egg and egg yolk in a small bowl. Combine sugar, cornstarch, and salt in a heavy medium saucepan. Stir in milk. Stirring constantly, cook over medium heat about 11 minutes or until mixture thickens; remove from heat. Stir 1/4 cup milk mixture into beaten eggs. Stirring constantly, add egg mixture back into hot mixture in saucepan; cook 2 minutes. Remove from heat; stir in vanilla. Spoon 1/2 cup filling into a separate bowl; stir in chocolate until melted. Pour chocolate mixture into crust. Place banana slices over chocolate mixture. Pour remaining filling over slices. Spread meringue over hot filling, sealing edges to crust. Bake 15 to 20 minutes or until meringue is golden brown. Cool completely on a wire rack. Store in an airtight container in refrigerator.

Yield: about 8 servings ❈

Chocolate-Mint Cheese Ball

1 package (6 ounces) semisweet chocolate chips

1 cup chopped pecans, toasted

2 packages (8 ounces each) cream cheese, softened

1/2 cup crushed 1" peppermint candies (about 18 candies or 3 1/2 ounces), divided

Chocolate wafer cookies to serve

In a blender or food processor, finely grind chocolate chips and pecans. In a medium bowl, combine chocolate chip mixture, cream cheese, and 1/4 cup crushed peppermints. Shape into a ball; wrap in plastic wrap and refrigerate until firm. Cover with remaining 1/4 cup crushed peppermints.

To serve, let stand at room temperature 20 to 30 minutes or until softened. Serve with cookies. **Yield:** 1 cheese ball ❄

Chocolate-Mint Cheese Ball

Old-Fashioned Christmas Spice Cookies

1 cup butter or margarine, softened
³/₄ cup sugar
1¹/₂ tablespoons dark molasses
2 teaspoons ground cinnamon
¹/₂ teaspoon ground cardamom or ginger
1 tablespoon water
1 teaspoon baking powder
2¹/₂ cups all-purpose flour
1 egg white, lightly beaten
Sugar

Beat butter at medium speed with an electric mixer until creamy. Add ³/₄ cup sugar, beating until smooth. Add molasses, cinnamon, and cardamom, beating until blended. Combine 1 tablespoon water and baking powder, stirring until baking powder is dissolved; add to butter mixture. Gradually add flour to butter mixture, beating until blended. Turn dough out onto a lightly floured surface; roll to ¹/₄" thickness. Cut with a 1¹/₂" round cookie cutter (or size to fit your tumbler). Place 2" apart on lightly greased baking sheets. Brush evenly with egg white; sprinkle with sugar. Bake in a preheated 375° oven for 8 minutes or until lightly browned. Cool on baking sheets 5 to 6 minutes. Remove to wire racks to cool completely.
Yield: about 7 dozen cookies ❊

Old-Fashioned Christmas Spice Cookies

Stack Old-Fashioned Christmas Spice Cookies in a tumbler for a thoughtful gift or party favor.

Creamy Cherry Brownies

1 jar (16 ounces) maraschino cherries, divided
1 package (22½ ounces) fudge brownie mix and ingredients to prepare brownies
1 package (3 ounces) cream cheese, softened
6 tablespoons butter or margarine, softened
2¼ cups confectioners sugar

Drain cherries, reserving syrup. Line a 9" x 13" baking pan with aluminum foil, extending foil over ends of pan; grease foil. To prepare brownie mix, use reserved syrup plus enough water to equal water measurement in recipe. In a large bowl, combine brownie mix and required ingredients; stir until blended. Stir in 1 cup cherries. Spread mixture into prepared pan. Bake in a preheated 350° oven for 27 to 30 minutes or until brownies begin to pull away from sides of pan and are firm. Cool in pan.

Finely chop remaining cherries; drain on paper towels and pat dry. In a medium bowl, beat cream cheese and butter until fluffy. Stir in confectioners sugar and chopped cherries. Spread icing over brownies. Cover and chill 2 hours or until icing is firm.

Lift brownies from pan using ends of foil. Cut into 2" squares. Store in an airtight container in refrigerator.
Yield: about 2 dozen brownies ❋

Maple Clusters

1 cup firmly packed brown sugar
1 cup granulated sugar
½ cup maple syrup
½ cup whipping cream
1 tablespoon light corn syrup
⅛ teaspoon salt
1 tablespoon butter or margarine
1 teaspoon vanilla extract
2 cups chopped walnuts

Butter sides of a heavy large saucepan. Combine sugars, maple syrup, whipping cream, corn syrup, and salt in pan. Stirring constantly, cook over medium-low heat until sugars dissolve. Using a pastry brush dipped in hot water, wash down any sugar crystals on sides of pan. Attach a candy thermometer to pan, making sure thermometer does not touch bottom of pan. Increase heat to medium and bring to a boil. Cook, without stirring, until mixture reaches 234°. Test about ½ teaspoon mixture in ice water. Mixture will easily form a ball in ice water but will flatten when held in your hand. Remove from heat and stir in butter and vanilla. Using medium speed of an electric mixer, beat until candy thickens and begins to lose it gloss (about 3 minutes). Stir in walnuts. Drop by teaspoonfuls onto waxed paper; cool completely. Store in an airtight container.
Yield: about 5 dozen candies ❋

Cranberry-Almond Supremes

1 cup butter, softened
¾ cup sugar
¾ cup firmly packed light brown sugar
½ teaspoon almond extract
2 large eggs
2¼ cups all-purpose flour
1 teaspoon baking powder
1 teaspoon salt
2 cups chopped fresh cranberries
1 cup slivered almonds, toasted

Beat butter at medium speed with an electric mixer until creamy; gradually add sugars, beating well. Add almond extract and eggs, beating until blended. Combine flour, baking powder, and salt; gradually add to butter mixture, beating at low speed until blended after each addition.

Stir in cranberries and almonds. Drop by rounded tablespoonfuls onto ungreased baking sheets. Bake in a preheated 375° oven for 9 to 11 minutes. Remove to wire racks to cool.
Yield: about 3½ dozen cookies ❋

Chocolate Petite Cheesecakes

Perfect for parties, Chocolate Petite Cheesecakes are individual servings that will disappear in a hurry!

Chocolate Petite Cheesecakes

Crust
1¾ cups chocolate graham cracker crumbs (about twelve 2½" x 5" crackers)
¼ cup butter or margarine, softened
2 tablespoons sugar

Filling
2 packages (8 ounces each) cream cheese, softened
¾ cup sugar
4 eggs
1 package (12 ounces) semisweet chocolate chips, melted
1 cup whipping cream
1 teaspoon vanilla extract
1 can (21 ounces) cherry pie filling

Line a muffin pan with aluminum foil muffin cups. For crust, combine graham cracker crumbs, butter, and sugar in a medium bowl. Press a tablespoon of mixture into bottom of each muffin cup.

For filling, beat cream cheese in a large bowl until fluffy. Gradually beat in sugar. Add eggs, one at a time, beating well after each addition. Beat in melted chocolate chips. Add whipping cream and vanilla; beat until smooth. Spoon about ¼ cup filling over crust in each muffin cup. Bake in a preheated 350° oven for 18 to 22 minutes or until centers are set. Cool in muffin pan. Remove cheesecakes from pan; chill overnight.

To serve, spoon 1 tablespoon pie filling in center of each cheesecake.

Yield: about 2 dozen cheesecakes ❋

helpful how-to's

❄ *general instructions* ❄

Sizing Patterns

To change the size of a pattern, divide the desired height or width of the pattern (whichever is larger) by the actual height or width of the pattern. Multiply the result by 100 and photocopy the pattern at this percentage.

For example: You want your pattern to be 8" high, but the pattern on the page is 6" high. So $8 \div 6 = 1.33 \times 100 = 133\%$. Copy the pattern at 133%.

Découpaging

Apply découpage glue to the wrong side of the paper, overlapping as neccessary. Arrange pieces on project and smooth in place; allow to dry.

Making Patterns

Place tracing paper over the pattern and draw over the lines. For a more durable pattern, use a permanent marker to draw over the pattern on stencil plastic.

Transferring Patterns To Fabrics

Pick the transfer method that works best with the fabric and project you've chosen. If you use a water-soluble pen, check first on a scrap piece to make sure the floss or felt colors won't bleed when you remove the pen markings.

Tissue Paper Method

Trace the pattern onto tissue paper. Pin the tissue paper to the felt or fabric and stitch through the paper. Carefully tear the tissue paper away.

Water-Soluble Marking Pen Method

Trace the pattern onto tracing paper. Tape the paper pattern and fabric to a sunny window; then, trace the pattern onto the fabric with the pen. Embroider the design. Lightly spritz the finished design with water to remove any visible pen markings.

Crochet

Abbreviations

ch(s)	chain(s)
cm	centimeters
dc	double crochet(s)
hdc	half double crochet
mm	millimeters
Rnd(s)	Round(s)
sc	single crochet(s)
sp(s)	space(s)
st(s)	stitch(es)
YO	yarn over

★ — work instructions following ★ as many **more** times as indicated in addition to the first time.

† to † — work all instructions from first † to second † as many times as specified.

( ) or [ ] — work enclosed instructions **as many** times as specified by the number immediately following **or** work all enclosed instructions in the stitch or space indicated **or** contains explanatory remarks.

GAUGE

Make a sample swatch in the thread/yarn and hook specified. Measure the swatch, counting stitches and rows or rounds carefully. If the swatch is larger or smaller than specified, make another, changing hook size to get the correct gauge.

Embroidery Stitches

Follow the stitch diagrams to bring the needle up at odd numbers and down at even numbers.

Blanket Stitch

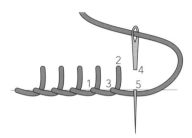

Fly Stitch

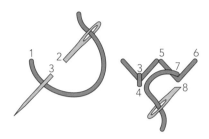

French Knot

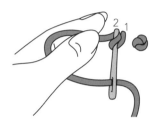

Lazy Daisy

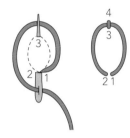

Running Stitch

Satin Stitch

Stem Stitch

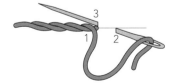

Straight Stitch

Making Pom-Poms

Cut a piece of cardboard 3" wide and as long as you want the diameter of your finished pom-pom to be. Wind the yarn around the cardboard (the more you wrap, the fluffier the pom-pom) *(Fig. 1a)*. Carefully slip the yarn off the cardboard and firmly tie an 18" length of yarn around the middle *(Fig. 1b)*. Leave yarn ends long enough to attach the pom-pom. Cut the loops on both ends and trim the pom-pom into a smooth ball *(Fig. 1c)*.

Fig. 1a

Fig. 1b

Fig. 1c

Using Jump Rings

To open a jump ring, use two pairs of needle-nose jewelry pliers to grasp the ring near each side of the opening. Pull one set of pliers toward you and push the other away to open the ring *(Fig. 2)*. Move the pliers the opposite way to close the ring. *(**Note:** Opening a jump ring by pulling the ends away from each other will weaken and distort the ring.)*

Fig. 2

Shaping Eye Loops

Grasp the end of a wire length or head pin with round-nose jewelry pliers *(Fig. 3a)*. Repositioning the pliers as needed, bend the wire end into a small loop *(Fig. 3b)*. Cut off any excess wire *(Fig. 3c)*. To open an eye loop, follow the instructions for opening a jump ring.

Fig. 3a

Fig. 3b

Fig. xc

Adding Crimp Beads

String a crimp bead on the wire. Place the bead on the inner groove of the crimping tool and squeeze *(Fig. 4a)*. Open the tool, turn the bead a quarter turn and place it in the outer groove of the tool. Squeeze to round out the bead *(Fig. 4b)*.

Fig. 4a

Fig. 4b

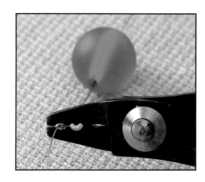

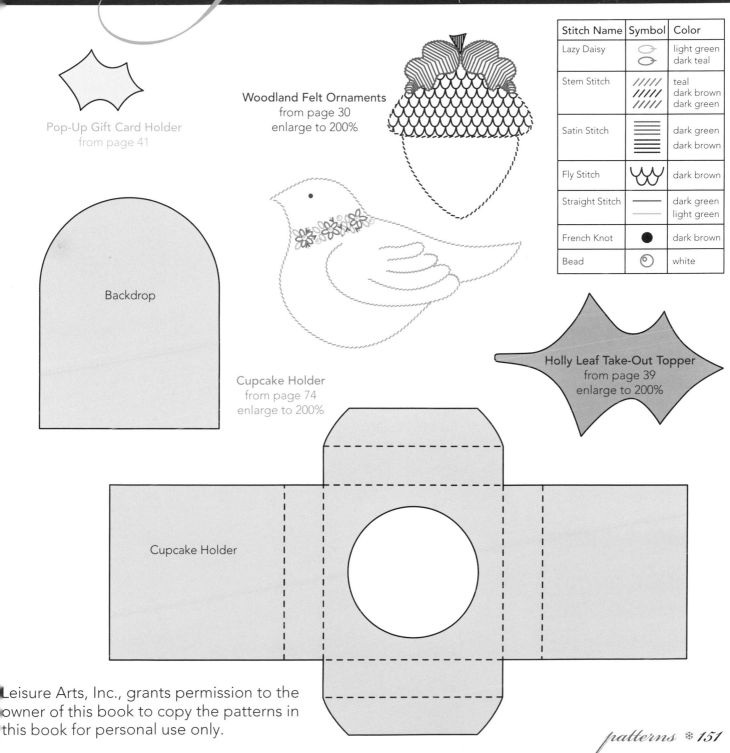

Pop-Up Gift Card Holder
from page 41

Woodland Felt Ornaments
from page 30
enlarge to 200%

Stitch Name	Symbol	Color
Lazy Daisy		light green
		dark teal
Stem Stitch	/////	teal
	/////	dark brown
	/////	dark green
Satin Stitch		dark green
		dark brown
Fly Stitch		dark brown
Straight Stitch		dark green
		light green
French Knot	●	dark brown
Bead	◎	white

Backdrop

Holly Leaf Take-Out Topper
from page 39
enlarge to 200%

Cupcake Holder
from page 74
enlarge to 200%

Cupcake Holder

Leisure Arts, Inc., grants permission to the owner of this book to copy the patterns in this book for personal use only.

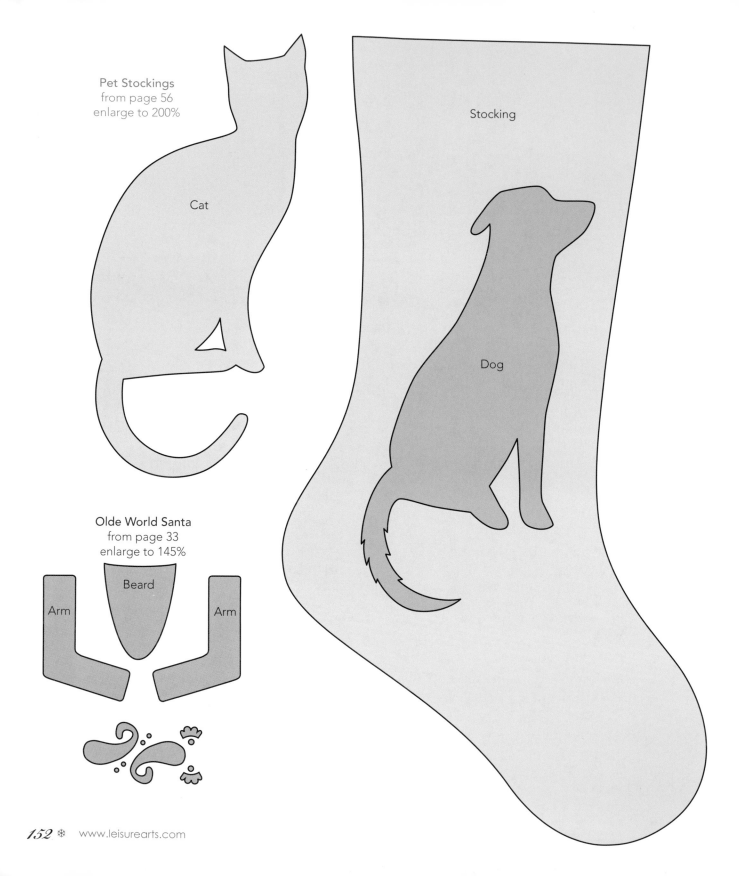

Pet Stockings
from page 56
enlarge to 200%

Cat

Stocking

Dog

Olde World Santa
from page 33
enlarge to 145%

Beard

Arm

Arm

Snowman Pincushion
from page 23
enlarge to 158%

Body

Nose

Arm

Base

Cheers-to-You Towel
from page 31
enlarge to 200%

Cheers

Stitch Key
■ ■ ■ Satin Stitch
// Stem Stitch
/// Straight Stitch
● French Knot

Tree Bag
from page 45
enlarge to 153%

Star

Tree and Ornaments

Cuff

Stocking

Posy

Posy
Center

Leaf

Daisy

Merry Mini Stockings
from page 60
enlarge to 131%

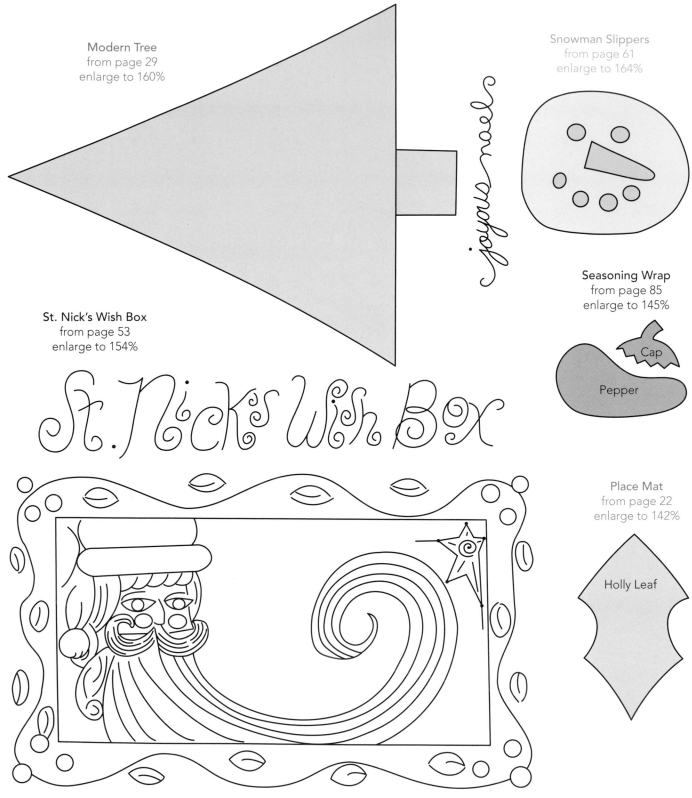

Modern Tree
from page 29
enlarge to 160%

Snowman Slippers
from page 61
enlarge to 164%

joyous noel

Seasoning Wrap
from page 85
enlarge to 145%

Cap

Pepper

St. Nick's Wish Box
from page 53
enlarge to 154%

St. Nick's Wish Box

Place Mat
from page 22
enlarge to 142%

Holly Leaf

Sparkling Snowflakes
from page 15
enlarge to 200%

Pretzel Glasses
from page 84
enlarge to 169%

Snowflake Topper
from page 39

Gift Sack
from page 77
enlarge to 150%

Flower

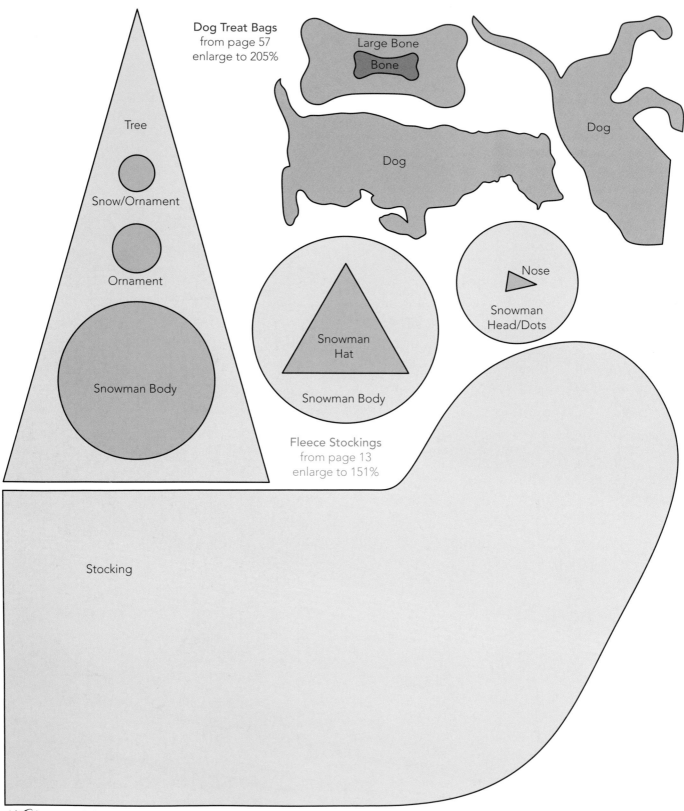

Tree

Snow/Ornament

Ornament

Snowman Body

Dog Treat Bags
from page 57
enlarge to 205%

Large Bone

Bone

Dog

Dog

Snowman Hat

Snowman Body

Nose

Snowman
Head/Dots

Fleece Stockings
from page 13
enlarge to 151%

Stocking

Bread Board Tag
from page 65
enlarge to 160%

garden herb
bread blend

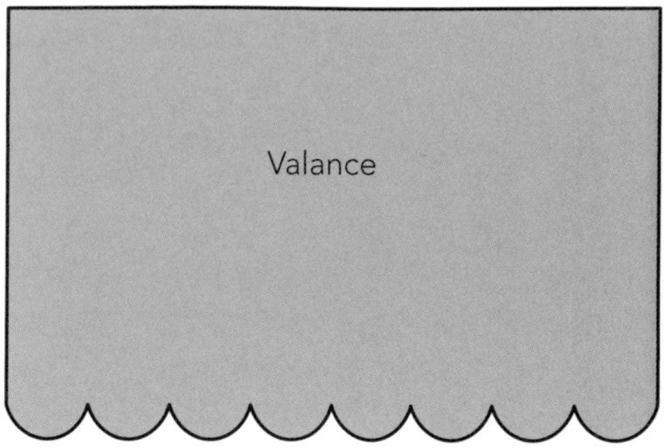

Valance

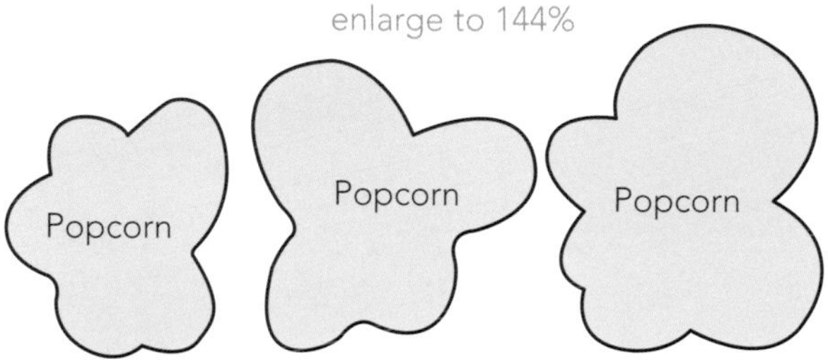

Cookie Holder
from page 69
enlarge to 142%

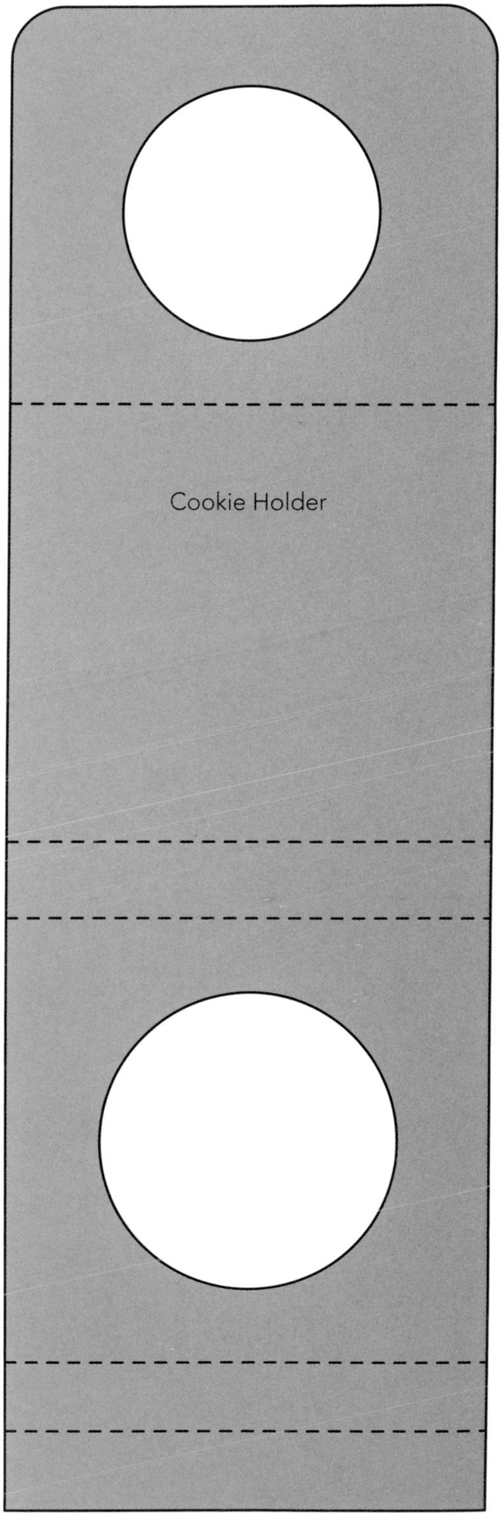

Popcorn Tin
from page 68
enlarge to 144%

Popcorn

Popcorn

Popcorn

Cookie Holder

Dog Coat
from page 55

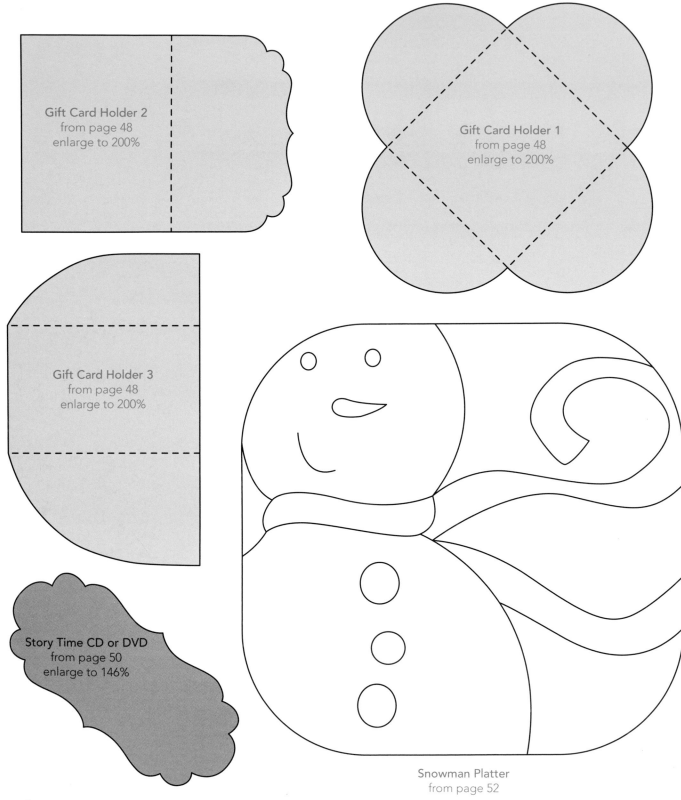

Gift Card Holder 2
from page 48
enlarge to 200%

Gift Card Holder 1
from page 48
enlarge to 200%

Gift Card Holder 3
from page 48
enlarge to 200%

Story Time CD or DVD
from page 50
enlarge to 146%

Snowman Platter
from page 52

❄ *project index* ❄

❄ recipe index ❄